Illinois Central College
Learning Resource Center

Studies in Language

STUDIES IN LANGUAGE

Noam Chomsky and Morris Halle, Editors

Cartesian Linguistics

Cartesian Linguistics

A CHAPTER IN THE
HISTORY OF RATIONALIST THOUGHT

NOAM CHOMSKY

Professor of Linguistics
Massachusetts Institute of Technology

HARPER & ROW, Publishers • New York and London

*P
123
.C53*

Cartesian Linguistics: A Chapter in the History of Rationalist Thought

LIBRARY OF CONGRESS CATALOG CARD NUMBER: 66-15670

Preface

The aim of this series of studies, of which the present work is the first, is to deepen our understanding of the nature of language and the mental processes and structures that underlie its use and acquisition. The idea that the study of language provides insight into human psychology is by no means novel. It has always been clear that the normal, everyday use of language involves intellectual abilities of the highest order. In view of the complexity of this achievement and its uniqueness to man, it is only natural to suppose that the study of language contributes significantly to our understanding of the nature of the human mind and its functioning.

Modern linguistics has provided a great deal of new information concerning a wide range and variety of languages. It has sought, with much success, to achieve significantly higher standards of clarity and reliability than those reached in earlier studies of language. At the same time, there has been a continuing interest in theoretical questions that has led to significant clarification of the foundations of linguistics. These advances make it possible to formulate, in a fairly precise way, the fundamental question of how experience and maturational processes interrelate within the framework of innate limiting conditions to yield the linguistic competence exhibited by a normal speaker of a language. It does not seem unrealistic, therefore, to hope that research of the sort that can be undertaken at present may lead to a plausible and informative account of the mental abilities that underlie the achievement of normal linguistic competence, abilities that may be as individual and species-specific as that of a bird to learn a particular class of songs, of a beaver to build dams, or of a bee to integrate its own actions into the intricate social activity of the hive.

The studies to be included in this series will be chosen for the light that they shed on the basic questions posed above. In selecting descriptive or theoretical works for the series, we shall ask ourselves, therefore, whether the linguistic data examined contribute to our understanding of the structures that underlie them, whether the linguistic structures exhibited provide insight into the general properties of human language, and whether the general properties of human language dealt with lead to inferences about the nature of the organism that is able to use and acquire language. Analogous considerations will guide our choice of historical and background studies. No such limitations will obtain regarding subject matter, for it is our express purpose to illustrate the full range of modern and traditional concerns with the problems of language.

From the point of view of subject matter the works to be included in the series may conveniently be grouped under three major headings: (1) investigations that focus directly on the nature of language, (2) studies dealing with the use of language and the abilities and mental organization that it presupposes, and (3) background studies placing the various approaches to the study of language in the appropriate historical and intellectual setting.

Under the first heading we plan to offer a number of studies that deal with specific aspects of individual languages. These will include descriptions of the syntax, semantics, and phonology of different languages as well as investigations into their evolution. Parallel to these we hope to issue several studies of the theoretical foundations on which the descriptive studies are based. Again, we expect to include works on grammar, semantics, and phonology, and an inquiry into the mechanism and causes of the still puzzling phenomenon of language change, which until a generation ago was the dominant subject of interest to linguists. Finally, to round out this part of the series, there will be a number of books on the purely formal aspects of language, envisaged as a mathematical object.

The second major grouping will, first of all, comprise studies in the psychology of language. We plan to include here attempts to develop models of language use, investigations into the perception of language and the effects of language on perception in general; studies of language learning both by children and by adults; and discussions of language pathology and various language surrogates, for example, the gesture language of the deaf. A second subclass in this category will be constituted by inquiries into the use of language for literary purposes; the study of the formal devices of poetry (meter, versification, etc.), of the syntactic features of prose style, and the semantic structure of narrative. Finally in a third subcategory we hope to publish works on the sociology of language, and the relation of language to and of its role in other forms of social interaction, such as ritual, kinship organization, magic, and art.

Among the background studies we hope to be able to include historical investigations of the technique of linguistic description, especially as it was practiced by the great forerunners of modern linguistics—the Sanskrit grammarians, the students of language in classical antiquity, in the middle ages (both Arabic and Western), and in more recent times. These will be contrasted with studies of a more philosophical bent, devoted to the deep intellectual connections that have always existed between the study of language, on the one hand, and theoretical psychology and the philosophy of the mind, on the other.

NOAM CHOMSKY

MORRIS HALLE

Acknowledgment

This research was completed while I was a fellow of the American Council of Learned Societies. It was supported in part by a grant from the National Institutes of Health (Grant No. MH-05120-04 and Grant No. MH-05120-05) to Harvard University, Center for Cognitive Studies. The collection of material was greatly facilitated by a grant from the Social Science Research Council.

Much of the material in this essay was presented in a series of Christian Gauss seminars at Princeton University in 1965. I am grateful to the participants for many useful comments. I am also indebted to William Bottiglia, Morris Halle, Roman Jakobson, Louis Kampf, Jerrold Katz, and John Viertel for very valuable suggestions and criticism.

NOAM CHOMSKY

Contents

A brief, and sufficiently accurate, description of the intellectual life of the European races during the succeeding two centuries and a quarter up to our own times is that they have been living upon the accumulated capital of ideas provided for them by the genius of the seventeenth century.

A. N. Whitehead, *Science and the Modern World*

Introduction

Whitehead's often quoted remark, cited above, provides a useful background for a discussion of the history of linguistics in the modern period. As applied to the theory of language structure, his assessment is quite correct with regard to the eighteenth and early nineteenth centuries. Modern linguistics, however, has self-consciously dissociated itself from traditional linguistic theory and has attempted to construct a theory of language in an entirely new and independent way. The contributions to linguistic theory of an earlier European tradition have in general been of little interest to professional linguists, who have occupied themselves with quite different topics within an intellectual framework that is not receptive to the problems that gave rise to earlier linguistic study or the insights that it achieved; and these contributions are by now largely unknown or regarded with unconcealed contempt. The few modern studies of the history of linguistics have typically taken the position that "tout ce qui est antérieur au XIXᵉ siècle, n'étant pas encore de la linguistique, peut être expédié en quelques lignes."[1] In recent years, there has been a noticeable reawakening of interest in questions that were, in fact, studied in a serious and fruitful way during the seventeenth, eighteenth, and early nineteenth centuries, though rarely since. Furthermore, this return to classical concerns has led to a rediscovery of much that was well understood in this period—what I will call the period of "Cartesian linguistics," for reasons that will be sketched below.

A careful study of the parallels between Cartesian linguistics and certain contemporary developments can be rewarding in many ways. A full account of them would go well beyond the scope of this essay, and any attempt to give such an account would, furthermore, be quite premature, in view of the sorry state of the field of the history of linguistics (itself in part a consequence of the disparagement of earlier work that has marked the modern period). I will limit myself here to something less ambitious, namely, a preliminary and fragmentary sketch of some of the leading ideas of Cartesian linguistics with no explicit analysis of its relation to current work that seeks to clarify and develop these ideas. The reader acquainted with current work in so-called "generative grammar" should have little difficulty in drawing these connections for himself.[2] Questions of current interest will, however, determine the general form of this sketch; that is, I will make no attempt to characterize Cartesian linguistics as it saw itself,[3] but rather will concentrate on the development of ideas that have reemerged, quite independently, in current work. My primary aim is simply to bring to the attention of those involved in the study of generative grammar and its implications some of the little-known work which has bearing on their concerns and problems and which often anticipates some of their specific conclusions.

This will be something of a composite portrait. There is no single individual who can be shown, on textual grounds, to have held all the views that will be sketched; perhaps Humboldt, who stands directly in the crosscurrents of rationalist and romanticist thought and whose work is in many ways the culmination as well as the terminal point of these developments, comes closest to this. Furthermore, the aptness of the term "Cartesian linguistics" for these developments in linguistic theory may well be questioned, on several grounds. First, these developments have roots in earlier linguistic work; second, several of the most active contributors to them would surely have regarded themselves as quite antagonistic to Cartesian doctrine (see note 3); third, Descartes himself devoted little attention to language, and his few remarks are subject to various interpretations. Each of these objections has some force. Still, it seems to me that there is, in the period under review here, a coherent and fruitful development of a body of ideas and conclusions regarding the nature of language in association with a certain theory of mind[4] and that this development can be regarded as an outgrowth of the Cartesian revolution. In any event, the aptness of the term is a matter of little interest. The important problem is to determine the exact nature of the "capital of ideas" accumulated in the premodern period, to evaluate the contemporary significance of this contribution, and to find ways to exploit it for advancing the study of language.

Creative Aspect of Language Use

Although Descartes makes only scant reference to language in his writings, certain observations about the nature of language play a significant role in the formulation of his general point of view. In the course of his careful and intensive study of the limits of mechanical explanation, which carried him beyond physics to physiology and psychology, Descartes was able to convince himself that all aspects of animal behavior can be explained on the assumption that an animal is an automaton.[5] In the course of this investigation, he developed an important and influential system of speculative physiology. But he arrived at the conclusion that man has unique abilities that cannot be accounted for on purely mechanistic grounds, although, to a very large extent, a mechanistic explanation can be provided for human bodily function and behavior. The essential difference between man and animal is exhibited most clearly by human language, in particular, by man's ability to form new statements which express new thoughts and which are appropriate to new situations. It is quite easy, in his view, to

> understand a machine's being constituted so that it can utter words, and even emit some responses to action on it of a corporeal kind, which brings about a change in its organs; for instance, if

it is touched in a particular part it may ask what we wish to say to it; if in another part it may exclaim that it is being hurt, and so on. But it never happens that it arranges its speech in various ways, in order to reply appropriately to everything that may be said in its presence, as even the lowest type of man can do.[6]

This ability to use language must not be confused with "natural movements which betray passions and may be imitated by machines as well as manifested by animals." The crucial difference is that automata "could never use speech or other signs as we do when placing our thoughts on record for the benefit of others." This is a specific human ability, independent of intelligence. Thus,

> it is a very remarkable fact that there are none so depraved and stupid, without even excepting idiots, that they cannot arrange different words together, forming of them a statement by which they make known their thoughts; while, on the other hand, there is no other animal, however perfect and fortunately circumstanced it may be, which can do the same.

Nor can this distinction between man and animal be based on peripheral physiological differences. Thus Descartes goes on to point out that

> it is not the want of organs that brings this to pass, for it is evident that magpies and parrots are able to utter words just like ourselves, and yet they cannot speak as we do, that is, so as to give evidence that they think of what they say. On the other hand, men who, being born deaf and dumb, are in the same degree, or even more than the brutes, destitute of the organs which serve the others for talking, are in the habit of themselves inventing certain signs by which they make themselves understood.

In short, then, man has a species-specific capacity, a unique type of intellectual organization which cannot be attributed to peripheral organs or related to general intelligence[7] and which manifests itself in what we may refer to as the "creative aspect" of ordinary language use—its property being both unbounded in scope and stimulus-free. Thus Descartes maintains that language is available for the free expression of thought or for appropriate response in any new context and is undetermined by any fixed association of utterances to external stimuli or physiological states (identifiable in any noncircular fashion).[8]

Arguing from the presumed impossibility of a mechanistic explanation for the creative aspect of normal use of language, Descartes concludes that in addition to body it is necessary to attribute mind—a substance whose essence is thought—to other humans. From the arguments that he offers for the association of mind to bodies that "bear a resemblance" to his, it seems clear that the postulated substance plays the role of a "creative principle" alongside of the "mechanical principle" that accounts for bodily function. Human reason, in fact, "is a universal instrument which can serve for all contingencies," whereas the organs of an animal or machine "have need of some special adaptation for any particular action."[9]

The crucial role of language in Descartes's argument is brought out still more clearly in his subsequent correspondence. In his letter to the Marquis of Newcastle (1646), he asserts that "there is no one of our external actions which can assure those who examine them that our body is anything more than a machine which moves of itself, but which also has in it a mind which thinks—excepting words, or other signs made in regard to whatever subjects present themselves, without reference to any passion."[10] The final condition is added to exclude "cries of joy or pain and the like" as well as "all that can be taught to any animal by art."[11] He goes on, then, to repeat the arguments in the *Discourse on Method*, emphasizing once again that there is no man so imperfect as not to use language for the expression of his thoughts and no "brute so perfect that it has made use of a sign to inform other animals of something which had no relation to their passions"; and, once again, pointing to the very perfection of animal instinct as an indication of lack of thought and as a

proof that animals are mere automata. In a letter of 1647 to Henry
More, he expresses himself in the following terms:

> But the principal argument, to my mind, which may convince
> us that the brutes are devoid of reason, is that, although among
> those of the same species, some are more perfect than others, as
> among men, which is particularly noticeable in horses and dogs,
> some of which have more capacity than others to retain what is
> taught them, and although all of them make us clearly understand
> their natural movements of anger, of fear, of hunger, and others
> of like kind, either by the voice or by other bodily motions, it
> has never yet been observed that any animal has arrived at such
> a degree of perfection as to make use of a true language; that is
> to say, as to be able to indicate to us by the voice, or by other
> signs, anything which could be referred to thought alone, rather
> than to a movement of mere nature; for the word is the sole sign
> and the only certain mark of the presence of thought hidden and
> wrapped up in the body; now all men, the most stupid and the
> most foolish, those even who are deprived of the organs of speech,
> make use of signs, whereas the brutes never do anything of the
> kind; which may be taken for the true distinction between man
> and brute.[12, 13]

In summary, it is the diversity of human behavior, its appropriateness to new situations, and man's capacity to innovate—
the creative aspect of language use providing the principle indication of this—that leads Descartes to attribute possession of
mind to other humans, since he regards this capacity as beyond
the limitations of any imaginable mechanism. Thus a fully adequate psychology requires the postulation of a "creative principle" alongside of the "mechanical principle" that suffices to
account for all other aspects of the inanimate and animate world
and for a significant range of human actions and "passions" as
well.

Descartes's observations on language in relation to the problem of mechanistic explanation were elaborated in an interesting
study by Cordemoy.[14] His problem in this study is to determine
whether it is necessary to assume the existence of other minds.[15]

A great deal of the complexity of human behavior is irrelevant to demonstrating that other persons are not mere automata, since it can be explained on hypothetical physiological terms, in terms of reflex and tropism. Limitations of such explanations are suggested by the fact that "ils s'approchent avec fermeté de ce qui les va détruire, et qu'ils abandonnent ce qui les pourroit conserver" (p. 7). This suggests that their actions are governed by a will, like his own. But the best evidence is provided by speech, by

> la liaison que je rencontre entre les Paroles que je leur entens proférer à tous momens (p. 8).

> Car encore que je conçoive bien qu'une pure machine pourroit proferer quelques paroles, je connois en mesme temps que si les ressorts qui distribûroient le vent, ou qui ferroient ouvrir les tuyaux, d'où ces voix sortiroient, avoient un certain ordre entr'eux, jamais ils ne le pourroient changer; de sorte que dés que la première voix seroit entenduë, celles qui auroient accoustumé de la suivre, le seroient necessairement aussi, pourveu que le vent ne manquât pas à la Machine: au lieu que les Paroles que j'entens proferer à des Corps faits comme le mien, n'ont presque jamais la mesme suite. J'observe d'ailleurs, que ces Paroles sont les mesmes, dont je me voudrois servir pour expliquer mes pensées à d'autres sujets, qui seroient capables de les concevoir. Enfin, plus je prens garde à l'effet que produisent mes Paroles, quand je les profère devant ces Corps, plus il me semble qu'elles sont entenduës; et celles qu'ils proferent répondent si parfaitement au sens des miennes, qu'il ne me paroist plus de sujet de douter qu'une Ame ne fasse en eux ce que la mienne fait en moy (pp. 8–10).

In short, Cordemoy is arguing that there can be no mechanistic explanation for the novelty, coherence, and relevance of normal speech. He emphasizes, however, that care must be exercised in using ability to speak as evidence for the inadequacy of mechanistic explanation. The fact that articulate sounds are produced or that utterances can be imitated in itself proves nothing, as this can be explained in mechanical terms. Nor is it of any relevance that "signes naturels" may be produced that express internal states or that specific signs may be produced that are contingent on the presence of external stimuli. It is only the ability to innovate, and to do so in a way which is appropriate to novel situations and which yields coherent discourse, that provides crucial evidence. "Parler n'est pas repeter les mesmes paroles dont on a eu l'oreille frappée, mais . . . c'est en proferer d'autres à propos de celles-là" (p. 19). To show that other persons are not automata, one must provide evidence that their speech manifests this creative aspect, that it is appropriate to whatever may be said by the "experimenter"; ". . . si je trouve par toutes les experiences que je suis capable d'en faire, qu'ils usent comme moy de la Parole, je croiray avoir une raison infaillible de croire qu'ils ont une Ame comme moy" (p. 21). Possible types of experiment are then outlined. For example, one can construct new "signes d'institution":

> je voy que je puis convenir avec quelques-uns d'eux, que ce qui signifie ordinairement une chose en signifiera une autre, et que cela reüssit de sorte, qu'il n'y a plus que ceux avec qui j'en suis convenu, qui me paroissent entendre ce que je pense (pp. 22–23).

Similarly, evidence is provided

> quand je verray que ces Corps feront des signes qui n'auront aucun rapport à l'estat où ils se trouveront, ny à leur conservation: quand je verray que ces signes conviendront à ceux que j'auray faits pour dire mes pensées; quand je verray qu'ils me donneront des idées que je n'avois pas auparavant, et qui se rapporteront à la chose que j'avois déja dans l'esprit; Enfin, quand je verray une grande suite entre leurs signes et les miens (pp. 28–29);

or by behavior that indicates "qu'ils avoient dessein de me tromper" (pp. 30–31). Under such circumstances, when many experiments of this sort have succeeded, "je ne seray pas raisonnable si je ne crois qu'ils le sont comme moy" (p. 29).

Throughout, what is stressed is the innovative aspect of intelligent performance. Thus,

. . . les nouvelles pensées, qui nous viennent par l'entretien que nous avons avec les hommes, sont un assuré témoignage à chacun de nous, qu'ils ont un esprit comme le nostre (p. 185);

. . . toute la raison que nous avons de croire qu'il y a des esprits unis aux corps des hommes qui nous parlent, est qu'ils nous donnent souvent de nouvelles pensées que nous n'avions pas, ou qu'ils nous obligent à changer celles que nous avions. . . . (p. 187).

Cordemoy consistently maintains that the "experiments" that reveal the limitations of mechanical explanation are those which involve the use of language, in particular, what we have called its creative aspect. In this, as in his discussion of the acoustic and articulatory basis for language use and the methods of conditioning, association, and reinforcement that may facilitate acquisition of true language by humans and nonlinguistic functional communication systems by animals, Cordemoy is working completely within the framework of Cartesian assumptions.

For our purposes what is important in this is the emphasis on the creative aspect of language use and on the fundamental distinction between human language and the purely functional and stimulus-bound animal communication systems, rather than the Cartesian attempts to account for human abilities.

It is noteworthy that subsequent discussion rarely attempts to meet the Cartesian arguments regarding the limitations of mechanical explanation. Descartes argued that a "thinking substance" must be postulated to account for the facts that he cites. This proposal is generally countered by the claim that a more complex organization of the body is sufficient to account for human abilities, but no serious attempt is made to show how this might be possible (as Descartes, Cordemoy, and others tried to show how animal behavior and human bodily functions of many kinds can be explained on the basis of assumptions about physical organization). La Mettrie, for example, holds that man is simply the most complex of machines. "He is to the ape, and to the most intelligent animals as the planetary pendulum of Huyghens is to a watch of Julien Leroy" (p. 140).[16] There is, in his opinion, no difficulty in accounting for thought on mechanical principles. "I believe that thought is so little incompatible with organized matter, that it seems to be one of its properties on a par with electricity, the faculty of motion, impenetrability, extension, etc." (pp. 143–144). There should, furthermore, be no obstacle in principle to teaching an ape to speak. It is only "some defect in the organs of speech" that stands in the way, and this can be overcome by proper training (p. 100). "I have very little doubt that if this animal were properly trained he might at last be taught to pronounce, and consequently to know a language. Then he would no longer be a wild man, nor a defective man, but he would be a perfect man, a little gentleman" (p. 103). Similarly, a talking machine is not beyond imagination. "Vaucanson, who needed more skill for making his flute player than for making his duck, would have needed still more to make a talking man, a mechanism no longer to be regarded as impossible . . ." (pp. 140–141).

Several years before the publication of *L'Homme Machine*, in a slight and presumably only semiserious work, Bougeant produced one of the very few attempts to refute explicitly the Cartesian argument that human and animal language differ in a fundamental way,[17] but his supposed counterargument merely reaffirms the Cartesian position regarding human and animal language. He bases his claim that "les Bêtes parlent et s'entendent entr'elles tout aussi-bien que nous et quelquefois mieux" (p. 4) on the grounds that they can be trained to respond to signals, that they exhibit their "divers sentimens" by external signs, that they can work in cooperation (for example, beavers, to whom he ascribes a language that has much in common with those "language games" that Wittgenstein regards as "primitive forms" of human language). However, he recognizes that "tout le langage des Bêtes se réduit à exprimer les sentimens de leurs passions, et on peut réduire toutes leurs passions à un petit nombre" (p. 152). "Il est nécessaire qu'elles repetent toujours la même expression,

et que cette répétition dure aussi longtemps que l'object les oc-
cupe" (p. 123). They have no "idées abstraites et metaphysiques":

> Elles n'ont que des connoissances directes absolument bornées
> à l'object présent et matériel qui frappe leurs sens. L'homme
> infiniment supérieur dans son langage, comme dans ses idées, ne
> sçauroit s'exprimer sans composer son discours de termes personnels
> et rélatifs, qui en déterminent le sens et l'application (p. 154).

Animals, in effect, have only names for various "passions qu'elles
sentent" (p. 155). They cannot produce "une phrase personifiée
et composée à notre manière" (p. 156):

> Pourquoi la nature a-t-elle donné aux Bêtes la faculté de parler?
> C'est uniquement pour exprimer entr'elles leurs désirs et leurs
> sentimens, afin de pouvoir satisfaire par ce moyen à leurs besoins
> et à tout ce qui est nécessaire pour leur conservation. Je sçais que
> le langage en général a encore un autre objet qui est d'exprimer
> les idées, les connoissances, les réfléxions, les raisonnemens. Mais
> quelque systême que l'on suive sur la connoissance des Bêtes, . . .
> il est certain que la nature ne leur a donné de connoissance que ce
> qui leur est utile ou nécessaire pour la conservation de l'espèce
> et de chaque individu. Point d'idées abstraites par conséquent,
> point de raisonnemens Métaphysiques, point de recherches curieuses
> sur tous les objets qui les environnent, point d'autre science que
> celle de se bien porter, de se bien conserver, d'éviter tout ce qui
> leur nuit, et de se procurer du bien. Aussi n'en a-t-on jamais vû
> haranguer en public, ni disputer des causes et de leurs effets. Elles
> ne connoissent que la vie animale (pp. 99–100).

In short, animal "language" remains completely within the bounds
of mechanical explanation as this was conceived by Descartes and
Cordemoy.

Evidently, neither La Mettrie nor Bougeant comes to grips with
the problem raised by Descartes—the problem posed by the creative aspect of language use, by the fact that human language,
being free from control by identifiable external stimuli or internal
physiological states, can serve as a general instrument of thought

and self-expression rather than merely as a communicative device of report, request, or command.[18] Modern attempts to deal with the problem of intelligent behavior are hardly more satisfactory. Ryle, for example, in his critique of "Descartes's myth"[19] simply avoids the issue entirely. He claims that the Cartesians should have been "asking by what criteria intelligent behavior is actually distinguished from non-intelligent behavior" (p. 21) rather than seeking an explanation for the former. Properly understood, these are not mutually exclusive alternatives. The criteria that Ryle discusses differ little, in principle, from Cordemoy's proposed "experiments"; but whereas Ryle is content simply to cite the fact that "intelligent behavior" has certain properties,[20] the Cartesians were concerned with the problem of accounting for such behavior in the face of their inability to provide an explanation in mechanical terms. It can hardly be claimed that we have advanced significantly beyond the seventeenth century in determining the characteristics of intelligent behavior, the means by which it is acquired, the principles that govern it, or the nature of the structures that underlie it. One may choose to ignore these problems, but no coherent argument has been offered that suggests that they are either unreal or beyond investigation.

Modern linguistics has also failed to deal with the Cartesian observations regarding human language in any serious way. Bloomfield, for example, observes that in a natural language "the possibilities of combination are practically infinite," so that there is no hope of accounting for language use on the basis of repetition or listing, but he has nothing further to say about the problem beyond the remark that the speaker utters new forms "*on the analogy* of similar forms which he has heard."[21] Similarly, Hockett attributes innovation completely to "analogy."[22] Similar remarks can be found in Paul, Saussure, Jespersen, and many others. To attribute the creative aspect of language use to "analogy" or "grammatical patterns" is to use these terms in a completely metaphorical way, with no clear sense and with no relation to the technical usage of linguistic theory. It is no less empty than

Ryle's description of intelligent behavior as an exercise of "powers" and "dispositions" of some mysterious sort, or the attempt to account for the normal, creative use of language in terms of "generalization" or "habit" or "conditioning." A description in these terms is incorrect if the terms have anything like their technical meanings, and highly misleading otherwise, in so far as it suggests that the capacities in question can somehow be accounted for as just a "more complicated case" of something reasonably well understood.

We have seen that the Cartesian view, as expressed by Descartes and Cordemoy as well as by such professed anti-Cartesians as Bougeant, is that in its normal use, human language is free from stimulus control and does not serve a merely communicative function, but is rather an instrument for the free expression of thought and for appropriate response to new situations.[23] These observations concerning what we have been calling the creative aspect of language use are elaborated in several ways in the eighteenth and early nineteenth centuries, as we shall see directly. At the same time, Descartes's second test for determining whether automata are "real men" is also reinterpreted, within the context of the "great chain of being." Descartes makes a sharp distinction between man and animal, arguing that animal behavior is a matter of instinct and that the perfection and specificity of animal instinct make it subject to mechanical explanation. A characteristic subsequent view is that there is a gradation of intelligence and that perfection of instinct varies inversely with intellectual ability. To La Mettrie, for example, it seems to be a universal law of nature "that the more one gains in intelligence (du côté de l'esprit), the more one loses in instinct" (p. 99). Cf. notes 7, 29.

The two Cartesian tests (possession of language, diversity of action) are interrelated by Herder, in an original way, in his influential Prize Essay on the origin of language.[24] Like Descartes, Herder argues that human language is different in kind from exclamations of passion and that it cannot be attributed to superior organs of articulation, nor, obviously, can it have its origins in imitation of nature or in an "agreement" to form language.[25] Rather, language is a natural property of the human mind. But nature does not provide man with an instinctive language, or an instinctive faculty of language, or a faculty of reason of which language is a "reflection." Man's fundamental quality is, rather, weakness of instinct, and man is clearly far inferior to animals in strength and certainty of instinct. But instinct and refinement of sense and skill correlate with narrowness of the scope and sphere of life and experience, with the focusing of all sensitivity and all power of representation on a narrow fixed area (pp. 15–16). The following can be taken as a general principle: "die Empfindsamkeit, die Fähigkeiten und Kunsttriebe der Tiere nehmen an Stärke und Intensität zu im umgekehrten Verhältnisse der Grösse und Mannigfaltigkeit ihres Wirkungskreises" (pp. 16–17). But man's faculties are less acute, more varied and more diffuse. "Der Mensch hat keine so einförmige und enge Sphäre, wo nur eine Arbeit auf ihn wartet . . ." (p. 17). He is not, in other words, under the control of external stimuli and internal drives and compelled to respond in a perfect and specific way. This freedom from instinct and from stimulus control is the basis for what we call "human reason"; ". . . wenn der Mensch Triebe der Tiere hätte, er das nicht haben könnte, was wir jetzt Vernunft in ihm nennen; denn eben diese Triebe rissen ja seine Kräfte so dunkel auf einen Punkt hin, dass ihm kein freier Besinnungskreis ward" (p. 22). It is this very weakness of instinct that is man's natural advantage, that makes him a rational being. ". . . wenn der Mensch kein instinktmässiges Tier sein sollte, er vermöge der freiwirkenden positiven Kraft seiner Seele ein besonnenes Geschöpf sein musste" (p. 22). In compensation for his weakness of instinct and sense, man receives the "Vorzug der Freiheit" (p. 20). "Nicht mehr eine unfehlbare Maschine in den Händen der Natur, wird er sich selbst Zweck und Ziel der Bearbeitung" (p. 20).

Free to reflect and to contemplate, man is able to observe, compare, distinguish essential properties, identify, and name. (Pp. 23f.) It is in this sense that language (and the discovery of language) is natural to man (p. 23), that "Der Mensch ist zum Sprachgeschöpf gebildet" (p. 43). On the one hand, Herder observes that man has no innate language—man does not speak by nature. On the other hand, language in his view is so specifically a product of man's particular intellectual organization that he is able to claim: "Könnte ich nun hier alle Enden zusammennehmen und mit einmal das Gewebe sichtbar machen, was menschliche Natur heisst: durchaus ein Gewebe zur Sprache." The resolution of the apparent paradox lies in his attempt to account for human language as a consequence of the weakness of human instinct.

Descartes had described human reason as "a universal instrument which can serve for all contingencies"[26] and which therefore provides for unbounded diversity of free thought and action.[27] Herder does not regard reason as a "faculty of the mind" at all but defines it rather as the freedom from stimulus control, and he attempts to show how this "natural advantage" makes it possible—in fact, necessary (p. 25)—for humans to develop language.

Somewhat before Herder, James Harris had given a characterization of "rationality" in terms rather similar to his, that is, as freedom from instinct rather than as a faculty with fixed properties. Harris distinguishes between the "*Human* Principle," which he calls "reason," and the "*Brutal* Principle," which he calls "instinct," in the following passage:

> MARK then . . . the Difference between *Human* Powers and *Brutal*—The Leading Principle of BRUTES appears to tend in each Species to *one single* Purpose—to this, in general, it *uniformly arrives;* and here, in general, it as *uniformly stops*—it needs no Precepts or Discipline to instruct it; nor will it easily be *changed,* or *admit a different Direction.* On the contrary, the Leading Principle of MAN is capable of *infinite* Directions—is convertible to *all sorts of Purposes*—equal to *all sorts of Subjects*—neglected, remains ignorant, and void of every Perfection—cultivated, becomes adorned with Sciences, and Arts—can raise us to excel, not only *Brutes,* but *our own Kind*—with respect to our *other* Powers and

Faculties, can instruct us how to *use* them, as well as *those* of the various *Natures*, which we see existing around us. In a word, to oppose the two Principles to each other—The Leading Principle of *Man*, is *Multiform*, *Originally Uninstructed*, *Pliant* and *Docil*— The Leading Principle of *Brutes* is *Uniform*, *Originally Instructed;* but, in most Instances afterward, *Inflexible* and *Indocil*.[28]

Thus we may say "that MAN is by Nature a RATIONAL ANIMAL," meaning by this nothing more than that he is free from the domination of instinct.[29]

A concern for the creative aspect of language use persists through the romantic period, in relation to the general problem of true creativity, in the full sense of this term.[30] A. W. Schlegel's remarks on language in his *Kunstlehre*[31] give a characteristic expression to these developments. In discussing the nature of language, he begins by observing that speech does not relate merely to external stimuli or goals. The words of language, for example, may arouse in the speaker and hearer ideas (Vorstellungen) of things that they have not directly perceived but know only by verbal description or that they "gar nicht sinnlich anschauen können, weil sie in der geistigen Welt ihr Dasein haben." Words may also designate abstracted properties and relations of the speaker to the hearer and to the topic of discourse, and relations among the elements of the latter. In combining our "Gedanken und Vorstellungen," we úse "Worte von so subtiler Bedeutung, dass es einen Philosophen in Verlegenheit setzen könnte, sie zu erklären." Still, they are used freely by the uninstructed and the unintelligent:

> Aus allem diesem fügen wir nun Reden zusammen, die den anderen nicht etwa bloss über äussere Zwecke verständigen, sondern ihn in das Innerste unseres Gemütes blicken lassen; wir erregen damit die mannigfaltigsten Leidenschaften, befestigen oder vernichten sittliche Entschlüsse, und entflammen eine versammelte Menge zu gemeinschaftlichen Regungen. Das Grösste wie das Kleinste, das Wunderbarste, nie Erhörte, ja das Unmögliche und Undenkbare gleitet mit gleicher Leichtigkeit über unsere Zunge.

So characteristic of language is this freedom from external control or practical end, for Schlegel, that he elsewhere[32] proposes that "alles, wodurch sich das Innere im äussern offenbart, mit Recht Sprache heisst."

From this conception of language, it is only a short step to the association of the creative aspect of language use with true artistic creativity.[33] Echoing Rousseau and Herder, Schlegel describes language as "die wunderbarste Schöpfung des menschlichen Dichtungsvermögens" (*Sprache und Poetik*, p. 145). Language is "ein immer werdendes, sich verwandelndes, nie vollendetes Gedicht des gesamten Menschengeschlechtes" (*Kunstlehre*, p. 226). This poetic quality is characteristic of the ordinary use of language, which "nie so gänzlich depoetisiert werden kann, dass sich nicht überall in ihr eine Menge zerstreute poetische Elemente finden sollten, auch bei dem willkürlichsten und kaltesten Verstandesgebrauch der Sprachzeichen, wieviel mehr im gemeinen Leben, in der raschen, unmittelbaren oft leidenschaftlichen Sprache des Umgangs" (*ibid.*, p. 228). There would have been little difficulty, he continues, in demonstrating to Moliere's M. Jourdain that he spoke poetry as well as prose.

The "poetical" quality of ordinary language derives from its independence of immediate stimulation (of "das körperlich wahrnehmbare Universum") and its freedom from practical ends. These characteristics, along with the boundlessness of language as an instrument of free self-expression, are essentially those emphasized by Descartes and his followers. But it is interesting to trace, in slightly greater detail, the argument by which Schlegel goes on to relate what we have called the creative aspect of language use to true creativity. Art, like language, is unbounded in its expressive potentiality.[34] But, Schlegel argues, poetry has a unique status among the arts in this respect; it, in a sense, underlies all the others and stands as the fundamental and typical art form. We recognize this unique status when we use the term "poetical" to refer to the quality of true imaginative creation in any of the arts. The explanation for the central position of poetry lies in its association with language. Poetry is unique in that its very medium is unbounded and free; that is, its medium, language, is a system with unbounded innovative potentialities for the formation and expression of ideas. The production of any work of art is preceded by a creative mental act for which the means are provided by language. Thus the creative use of language, which, under certain conditions of form and organization, constitutes poetry (cf. p. 231), accompanies and underlies any act of the creative imagination, no matter what the medium in which it is realized. In this way, poetry achieves its unique status among the arts, and artistic creativity is related to the creative aspect of language use.[35] Compare Huarte's third kind of wit—see note 9.

Schlegel distinguishes human from animal language in the typical Cartesian manner. Thus he observes that one cannot attribute man's linguistic ability to the "Anlage seiner Organe":

> Verschiedene Tierarten teilen sie in einem gewissen Grade mit ihm, und können, wiewohl ganz mechanisch, sprechen lernen. Es wird nämlich durch Nötigung und häufige Wiederholung in ihre Organe ein Reiz zu gewissen Bewegungen gebracht; sie gebrauchen aber die erlernten Wörter niemals selbsttätig (wenn es auch so scheinen sollte), um etwas damit zu bezeichnen, und es ist also ebensowenig ein eigentliches Sprechen als die Laute, welche eine Sprechmaschine hervorbringt (p. 236).

We cannot draw analogies between human and animal intellectual function. Animals live in a world of "Zustände," not of "Gegenstände" in the human sense (the same is true, in part, of young children, which accounts for the confused and incoherent character of even the liveliest childhood memories). The "tierische Abhängigkeit" is, for Schlegel, sharply opposed to the "selbsttätige Prinzip," the principle of "verständige Willkür," which characterizes human mental life. It is this principle that provides the basis for human language. It leads to a search for coherence and unity in experience, to comparison of sensible impressions (which requires mental signs, of some sort), and to the unique human capacity and need "auch dasjenige durch Sprache bezeichnen zu wollen, was in keiner sinnlichen Anschauung gegeben werden kann." What results is a human language, which serves primarily "als Gedankenorgans, als eines Mittels, selbst zur Besinnung zu gelangen," and only derivatively for the purposes of "geselligen Mitteilung" (pp. 237–241).

The Cartesian emphasis on the creative aspect of language use, as the essential and defining characteristic of human language, finds its most forceful expression in Humboldt's attempt to develop a comprehensive theory of general linguistics.[36] Humboldt's characterization of language as *energeia* ("Thätigkeit") rather than *ergon* ("Werk"),[37] as "eine Erzeugung" rather than "ein todtes Erzeugtes," extends and elaborates—often, in almost the same words—the formulations typical of Cartesian linguistics and romantic philosophy of language and aesthetic theory. For Humboldt, the only true definition of language is "eine genetische": "Sie ist nämlich die sich ewig wiederholende *Arbeit des Geistes*, den *articulirten Laut*[38] zum Ausdruck des Gedanken fähig zu machen" (p. 57). There is a constant and uniform factor underlying this "Arbeit des Geistes"; it is this which Humboldt calls the "Form" of language.[39] It is only the underlying laws of generation that are fixed, in language. The scope and manner in which the generative process may operate in the actual production of speech (or in speech perception, which Humboldt regards as a partially analogous performance—see pp. 70–72, below) are totally undetermined. See note 38.

The concept of Form includes the "Regeln der Redefügung" as well as the rules of "Wortbildung" and the rules of formation of concepts that determine the class of "Grundwörter" (p. 61). In contrast, the Substance ("Stoff") of language is unarticulated sound and "die Gesamtheit der sinnlichen Eindrücke und selbstthätigen Geistesbewegungen, welche der Bildung des Begriffs mit Hülfe der Sprache vorausgehen" (p. 61). The Form of language is a systematic structure. It contains no individual elements as isolated components but incorporates them only in so far as "eine Methode der Sprachbildung" can be discovered in them (p. 62).

The fixed mechanisms that, in their systematic and unified representation, constitute the form of the language must enable it to produce an indefinite range of speech events corresponding to the conditions imposed by thought processes. The domain of language is infinite and boundless, the "Inbegriff alles Denkbaren" (p. 122). Consequently, the fundamental property of a language must be its capacity to use its finitely specifiable mechanisms for an unbounded and unpredictable set of contingencies. "Sie muss daher von endlichen Mitteln einen unendlichen Gebrauch machen, und vermag dies durch die Identität der Gedanken und Sprache erzeugenden Kraft" (p. 122).

Not even the lexicon of a language can, according to Humboldt, be regarded as a "fertig daliegende Masse." Even apart from the formation of new words, the use of the lexicon by the speaker or the hearer involves "ein fortgehendes Erzeugniss und Wiedererzeugniss des wortbildenden Vermögens" (pp. 125–126). This is true of the original formation of the language and its acquisition by children, and it is also true of the daily use of speech (cf. note 25). He thus regards the lexicon, not as a memorized list from which words are simply extracted as language is used ("kein menschliches Gedächtniss reichte dazu hin, wenn nicht die Seele instinctartig zugleich den Schlüssel zur Bildung der Wörter selbst in sich trüge"), but rather as based on certain organizing generative principles that produce the appropriate items on given occasions. It is from such an assumption that he develops his well-known view that (in modern terms) concepts are organized in terms of certain "semantic fields" and that they receive their "value" in terms of their relation to the principles that determine this system.

Speech is an instrument of thought and self-expression. It plays an "immanent" and "constitutive" role in determining the nature of man's cognitive processes, his "denkende und im Denken schöpferische Kraft" (p. 36), his "Weltanschauung" and processes of "Gedankenverknüpfung" (p. 50). More generally, a human language as an organized totality is interposed between man and "die innerlich und äusserlich auf ihn einwirkende Natur" (p. 74). Although languages have universal properties, attributable to human mentality as such, nevertheless each language provides a "thought world" and a point of view of a unique sort. In attributing such a role in the determination of mental processes to individual languages, Humboldt departs radically from the framework of Cartesian linguistics, of course, and adopts a point of view that is more typically romantic.

Humboldt does remain within the Cartesian framework, however, in so far as he regards language primarily as a means of thought and self-expression rather than as an animal-like functional communication system—when he maintains, for example, that man "umgiebt sich mit einer Welt von Lauten, um die Welt von Gegenständen in sich aufzunehmen und zu bearbeiten" (p. 70). Thus even in its beginnings, "die Sprache dehnt sich absichtlos auf alle Gegenstände zufälliger sinnlicher Wahrnehmung und innerer Bearbeitung aus" (p. 75). He regards it as a mistake to attribute language primarily to the need for mutual assistance. "Der Mensch ist nicht so bedürftig, und zur Hülfsleistung hätten unarticulirte Laute ausgereicht" (p. 75). There are, to be sure, purely practical uses of language, as, for example, if a man orders a tree to be felled and "denkt sich nichts, als den bezeichneten Stamm, bei dem Worte" (p. 220). The same words might, however, have a "gesteigerte Geltung" if they were used in a description of nature or in a poem, for example, in which case the words are not used simply as instruments or with a purely referential function, are not used "mit *vereinzelter Seelenthätigkeit* einseitig zu einem abgeschlossnen *Zwecke*," but are rather referred to "ein inneres Ganzes des Gedankenzusammenhanges und der Empfindung" (p. 221). It is only in the latter case that the full resources of language are used in forming or interpreting speech, that all aspects of the lexical and grammatical structure of an utterance make their full contribution to its interpretation.

The purely practical use of language is characteristic of no real human language, but only of invented parasitic systems.[40]

In developing the notion of "form of language" as a generative principle, fixed and unchanging, determining the scope and providing the means for the unbounded set of individual "creative" acts that constitute normal language use, Humboldt makes an original and significant contribution to linguistic theory—a contribution that unfortunately remained unrecognized and unexploited until fairly recently.[41] The nature of Humboldt's contribution can be appreciated by comparing his notion of "form" to that developed in Harris's *Hermes* (1751), for example. For Harris, a language is essentially a system of words. Their meanings (the ideas of which they are the symbols) constitute the form of language; their sound, its matter (substance). Harris's notion of form is modeled on a classical pattern, the underlying conception being that of shape or orderly arrangement. But in his work on language, Harris does not suggest that a description of its form requires more than a specification of elements, categories, and the association of "content elements" to "expression elements." He does not, in other words, give any indication of grasping Humboldt's insight that language is far more than "patterned organization" of elements of various types and that any adequate description of it must refer these elements to the finite system of generative principles which determine the individual linguistic elements and their interrelations and which underlie the infinite variety of linguistic acts that can be meaningfully performed.[42]

The development of Humboldt's notion of "form of language" must be considered against the background of the intensive discussion during the romantic period of the distinction between "mechanical form" and "organic form." A. W. Schlegel makes the distinction in the following way:

> Form is mechanical when, through external force, it is imparted to any material merely as an accidental addition without reference

to its quality; as, for example, when we give a particular shape
to a soft mass that it may retain the same after its induration.
Organical form, again, is innate; it unfolds itself from within,
acquires its determination contemporaneously with the perfect
development of the germ.[43]

In Coleridge's paraphrase:

> The form is mechanic, when on any given material we impress
> a pre-determined form, not necessarily arising out of the properties
> of the material;—as when to a mass of wet clay we give whatever
> shape we wish it to retain when hardened. The organic form,
> on the other hand, is innate; it shapes, as it develops, itself from
> within, and the fulness of its development is one and the same
> with the perfection of its outward form. Such as the life is, such
> is the form. Nature, the prime genial artist, inexhaustible in diverse
> powers, is equally inexhaustible in forms;—each exterior is the
> physiognomy of the being within,—its true image reflected and
> thrown out from the concave mirror. . . .[44]

The context, in both cases, is an investigation of how individual
works of genius are constrained by rule and law. Humboldt's
concept of the "organic form" of language, and its role in determining the individual creations of speech, is a natural by-product
of the discussion of organic and mechanical form, particularly,
in the light of the connection that had already been drawn between artistic creativity and the creative aspect of language use
(cf. pp. 17–18, above).[45]

The parallel between Humboldt's notion of "organic form" in
language and Goethe's much earlier theory of "Urform" in
biology[46] is also quite striking. The concept of "Urform" was
intended as a new dimension beyond the "static" concept of form
of Linneaus and Cuvier, for example (namely, the concept of
form as structure and organization). But, at least at one stage of
his thought, Goethe took this dimension to be one of logical
rather than temporal order. In a letter to Herder, in 1787, Goethe
writes:

Die Urpflanze wird das wunderlichste Geschöpf von der Welt,
um welches mich die Natur selbst beneiden soll. Mit diesem Modell
und dem Schlüssel dazu kann man alsdann noch Pflanzen ins
Unendliche erfinden, die konsequent sein müssen, das heisst, die,
wenn sie auch nicht existieren, doch existieren könnten, und nicht
etwa mahlerische oder dichterische Schatten and Scheine sind,
sondern eine innerliche Wahrheit und Nothwendigkeit haben.
Dasselbe Gesetz wird sich auf alles übrige Lebendige anwenden
lassen.[47]

Thus, the Urform is a kind of generative principle that determines the class of physically possible organisms; and, in elab-
orating this notion, Goethe tried to formulate principles of
coherence and unity which characterize this class and which can
be identified as a constant and unvarying factor beneath all the
superficial modifications determined by variation in environ-
mental conditions. (Cf. Magnus, *op. cit.*, chap. 7, for some relevant material.) In a similar way, Humboldt's "linguistic form"
constrains all individual acts of speech production or perception
in a particular language, and, more generally, the universal aspects of grammatical form determine the class of possible languages.[48]

Finally, we should note that Humboldt's conception of language must be considered against the background provided by his
writings on social and political theory[49] and the concept of human
nature that underlies them. Humboldt has been described as "the
most prominent representative in Germany" of the doctrine of
natural rights and of the opposition to the authoritarian state.[50]
His denunciation of excessive state power (and of any sort of
dogmatic faith) is based on his advocacy of the fundamental
human right to develop a personal individuality through mean-
ingful creative work and unconstrained thought:

Naturally, freedom is the necessary condition without which
even the most soul-satisfying occupation cannot produce any
wholesome effects of this sort. Whatever task is not chosen of
man's free will, whatever constrains or even only guides him, does

not become part of his nature. It remains forever alien to him; if he performs it, he does so not with true humane energy but with mere mechanical skill (Cowan, *op. cit.*, pp. 46–47).

> [Under the condition of freedom from external control] . . . all peasants and craftsmen could be transformed into *artists*, i.e., people who love their craft for its own sake, who refine it with their self-guided energy and inventiveness, and who in so doing cultivate their own intellectual energies, ennoble their character, and increase their enjoyments. This way humanity would be ennobled by the very things which now, however beautiful they might be, degrade it (*ibid.*, p. 45).

The urge for self-realization is man's basic human need (as distinct from his merely animal needs). One who fails to recognize this "ought justly to be suspected of failing to recognize human nature for what it is and of wishing to turn men into machines" (*ibid.*, p. 42). But state control is incompatible with this human need. It is fundamentally coercive, and therefore "it produces monotony and uniformity, and alienates people's actions from their own character" (*ibid.*, p. 41; "so bringt er Einformigkeit und eine fremde Handlungsweise"). This is why "true reason cannot desire for man any condition other than that in which . . . every individual enjoys the most absolute, unbounded freedom to develop himself out of himself, in true individuality" (*ibid.*, p. 39). On the same grounds, he points to the "pernicious results of limitations upon freedom of thought" and "the harm done if the government takes a positive promoting hand in the business of religious worship" (*ibid.*, pp. 30–31), or if it interferes in higher education (*ibid.*, p. 133f.), or if it regulates personal relations of any sort (e.g., marriage; *ibid.*, p. 50), and so on. Furthermore, the rights in question are intrinsically human and are not to be limited to "the few in any nation"; "there is something utterly degrading to humanity in the very thought that some human being's right to be human could be abrogated" (*ibid.*, p. 33). To determine whether the fundamental human rights are being honored, we must consider, not just what a person does, but the conditions under which he does it—whether it is done under external control or spontaneously, to fulfill an inner need. If a man acts in a purely mechanical way, "we may admire what he does, but we despise what he is" (*ibid.*, p. 37).[51]

It is clear, then, that Humboldt's emphasis on the spontaneous and creative aspects of language use derives from a much more general concept of "human nature," a concept which he did not originate but which he developed and elaborated in original and important ways.

As remarked above, Humboldt's effort to reveal the organic form of language—the generative system of rules and principles that determines each of its isolated elements—had little impact on modern linguistics, with one significant exception. The structuralist emphasis on language as "un système òu tout se tient" is conceptually, at least, a direct outgrowth of the concern for organic form in Humboldtian linguistics. For Humboldt, a language is not to be regarded as a mass of isolated phenomena—words, sounds, individual speech productions, etc.—but rather as an "organism" in which all parts are interconnected and the role of each element is determined by its relation to the generative processes that constitute the underlying form. In modern linguistics, with its almost exclusive restriction of attention to inventories of elements and fixed "patterns" the scope of "organic form" is far more narrow than in the Humboldtian conception. But within this more narrow frame, the notion of "organic interconnection" was developed and applied to linguistic materials in a way that goes far beyond anything suggested in Humboldt. For modern structuralism, the dominant assumption is that "un système phonologique [in particular] n'est pas la somme mécanique de phonèmes isolés, mais un tout organique dont les phonèmes sont les membres et dont la structure est soumise à des lois."[52] These further developments are familiar, and I will say nothing more about them here.

As noted above, the form of language, for Humboldt, embraces the rules of syntax and word formation as well as the sound sys-

tem and the rules that determine the system of concepts that constitute the lexicon. He introduces a further distinction beween
the form of a language and what he calls its "character." It seems
to me that, as he employs this term, the character of a language
is determined by the manner in which it is used, in particular, in
poetry and philosophy; and the "inner character" (p. 208) of a
language must be distinguished from its syntactic and semantic
structure, which are matters of form, not use. "Ohne die Sprache
in ihren Lauten, und noch weniger in ihren Formen und Gesetzen
zu verändern, führt die *Zeit* durch wachsende Ideenentwickelung,
gesteigerte Denkkraft und tiefer eindringendes Empfindungsvermögen oft in sie ein, was sie früher nicht besass" (p. 116). Thus
a great writer or thinker can modify the character of the language and enrich its means of expression without affecting its
grammatical structure. The character of a language is closely
related to other elements of the national character and is a highly
individual creation. For Humboldt, as for his Cartesian and
romantic precursors, the normal use of language typically involves
creative mental acts; but it is the character of a language rather
than its form that reflects true "creativity" in a higher sense—
in the sense that implies value as well as novelty.

For all his concern with the creative aspect of language use and
with form as generative process, Humboldt does not go on to
face the substantive question: what is the precise character of
"organic form" in language. He does not, so far as I can see,
attempt to construct particular generative grammars or to determine the general character of any such system, the universal
schema to which any particular grammar conforms. In this respect, his work in general linguistics does not reach the levels
achieved by some of his predecessors, as we shall see directly. His
work is also marred by unclarity regarding several fundamental
questions, in particular, regarding the distinction between the
rule-governed creativity which constitutes the normal use of
language and which does not modify the form of the language
at all and the kind of innovation that leads to a modification in

the grammatical structure of the language. These defects have been recognized and, to some extent, overcome in more recent work. Furthermore, in his discussion of generative processes in language it is often unclear whether what he has in mind is underlying competence or performance—Aristotle's first or second grade of actuality of form (*De Anima*, book II, chap. 1). This classical distinction has been reemphasized in modern work. See note 2, and references given there. The concept of generative grammar, in the modern sense, is a development of the Humboldtian notion of "form of language" only if the latter is understood as form in the sense of "possession of knowledge" rather than "actual exercise of knowledge," in Aristotelian terms. See note 39.

It should, incidentally, be noted that the failure to formulate rules of sentence construction in a precise way was not simply an oversight of Cartesian linguistics. To some extent it was a consequence of the express assumption that the sequence of words in a sentence corresponds directly to the flow of thought, at least in a "well-designed" language,[53] and is therefore not properly studied as part of grammar. In the *Grammaire générale et raisonnée* it is maintained that, except for the figurative use of language, there is little to be said in grammar regarding rules of sentence construction (p. 145). In Lamy's rhetoric, shortly after, omission of any discussion of "l'ordre des mots, et les règles qu'il faut garder dans l'arrangement du discours" is justified on the grounds that "la lumière naturelle montre si vivement ce qu'il faut faire" that no further specification is necessary (p. 25).[54] At about the same time, Bishop Wilkins[55] distinguishes those constructions that are merely "customary" (*take one's heels and fly away, hedge a debt, be brought to heel*, etc.) from those which follow the "natural sense and order of the words" and therefore need no special discussion (p. 354); for example, the arrangement of Subject, Verb, and Object, or Subject, Copula, and Adjective, or the ordering of "grammatical" and "transcendental" particles relative to the items they govern, etc. (p. 354).

At the opposite pole from the belief in "natural order" is the view that each language contains an arbitrary collection of "patterns" learned through constant repetition (and "generalization") and forming a set of "verbal habits" or "dispositions." The belief that language structure and language use can somehow be described in these terms underlies much of the modern study of language and verbal behavior, often coupled with a denial of the possibility of useful cross-linguistic generalizations in syntax (see pp. 12–13, above). Like the reliance on a presumed natural order, it has helped foster a neglect of the problem of specifying the "grammatical form" of particular languages or the general abstract schema to which each language must conform.[56]

In summary, one fundamental contribution of what we have been calling "Cartesian linguistics" is the observation that human language, in its normal use, is free from the control of independently identifiable external stimuli or internal states and is not restricted to any practical communicative function, in contrast, for example, to the pseudo language of animals. It is thus free to serve as an instrument of free thought and self-expression. The limitless possibilities of thought and imagination are reflected in the creative aspect of language use. The language provides finite means but infinite possibilities of expression constrained only by rules of concept formation and sentence formation, these being in part particular and idiosyncratic but in part universal, a common human endowment. The finitely specifiable form of each language—in modern terms, its generative grammar (cf. note 39)—provides an "organic unity" interrelating its basic elements and underlying each of its individual manifestations, which are potentially infinite in number.

The dominant view throughout this period is that "les langues sont le meilleur miroir de l'esprit humain."[57] This virtual identification of linguistic and mental processes is what motivates the Cartesian test for the existence of other minds, discussed above. It finds expression throughout the romantic period. For Friedrich Schlegel, "so unzertrennlich ist Geist und Sprache, so wesentlich

Eins Gedanke und Wort, dass wir, so gewiss wir den Gedanken als das eigentümliche Vorrecht des Menschen betrachten, auch das Wort, nach seiner innern Bedeutung und Würde als das ursprüngliche Wesen des Menschen nennen können."[58] We have already made reference to Humboldt's conclusion that the force that generates language is indistinguishable from that which generates thought. Echoes of this conclusion persist for some time,[59] but they become less frequent as we enter the modern period.

The association of language and mind, it should be noted, is regarded rather differently in the earlier and later phases of the period under review. The earlier view is that the structure of language reflects the nature of thought so closely that "la science de la parole ne diffère guère de celle de la pensée" (Beauzée, p. x)[60]; the creative aspect of language use is accounted for on the basis of this assumption.[61] On the other hand, the observation that language serves as a medium of thought begins to be rephrased as the view that language has a constitutive function with respect to thought. La Mettrie, for example, in discussing how the brain compares and relates the images that it discerns, concludes that its structure is such that, once the signs of objects and their differences "have been traced or imprinted on the brain, the soul necessarily examines their relations[62]—an examination that would have been impossible without the discovery of signs or the invention of language" (op. cit., p. 105); prior to the discovery of language, things could only be perceived in a vague or superficial way. We have already refered to Humboldt's view that "Der Mensch lebt mit den Gegenständen hauptsächlich, ja, da Empfinden und Handeln in ihm von seinen Vorstellungen abhängen, sogar ausschliesslich so, wie die Sprache sie ihm zuführt" (op. cit., p. 74). Under the impact of the new relativism of the romantics, the conception of language as a constitutive medium for thought undergoes a significant modification, and the notion that language difference can lead to differences, even incomparability in mental processes, is explored.[63] This development, however, is not part of our main theme; its modern elaboration is familiar, and I will discuss it no further here.

Deep and Surface Structure

We have observed that the study of the creative aspect of language use develops from the assumption that linguistic and mental processes are virtually identical, language providing the primary means for free expression of thought and feeling, as well as for the functioning of the creative imagination. Similarly, much of the substantive discussion of grammar, throughout the development of what we have been calling "Cartesian linguistics," derives from this assumption. The Port-Royal *Grammar*, for example, begins the discussion of syntax with the observation that there are "trois operations de nostre esprit: concevoir, juger, raisonner" (p. 27), of which the third is irrelevant to grammar (it is taken up in the Port-Royal *Logic*, which appeared two years later, in 1662). From the manner in which concepts are combined in judgments, the *Grammar* deduces what it takes to be the general form of any possible grammar, and it proceeds to elaborate this universal underlying structure from a consideration of "la manière naturelle en laquelle nous exprimons nos pensées" (p. 30).[64] Most subsequent attempts to develop a schema of universal grammar proceed along the same lines.

James Harris's *Hermes*, which does not bear the imprint of the Port-Royal *Grammar* to the extent usual in eighteenth-century work, also reasons from the structure of mental processes to the structure of language, but in a somewhat different way. In general, he maintains, when a man speaks, "his Speech or Discourse is *a publishing of some Energie or Motion of his soul*" (p. 223).[65] The "powers of the soul" are of two general types: perception (involving the senses and the intellect) and volition (the will, passions, appetites—"all that moves to Action whether rational or irrational" (p. 224)). It follows that there are two kinds of linguistic acts: to assert, that is, "to publish some Perception either of the Senses or the Intellect"; or to "publish volitions," that is, to interrogate, command, pray, or wish (p. 224). The first type of sentence serves "to declare ourselves to others"; the second, to induce others to fulfill a need. Continuing in this way, we can analyze the volitional sentences in terms of whether the need is "to have some perception informed" or "some volition gratified" (the interrogative and requisitive modes, respectively); the requisitive is further analyzed as imperative or precative, depending on whether the sentence is addressed to inferiors or non-inferiors). Since both interrogatives and requisitives serve "to answer to a need," both types "require a return"—a return in words or deeds, to the requisitive, and in words alone, to the interrogative (p. 293f.).[66] Thus the framework for the analysis of types of sentences is provided by a certain analysis of mental processes.

Pursuing the fundamental distinction between body and mind, Cartesian linguistics characteristically assumes that language has two aspects. In particular, one may study a linguistic sign from the point of view of the sounds that constitute it and the characters that represent these signs or from the point of view of their "signification," that is, "la manière dont les hommes s'en servent pour signifier leurs pensées" (*Grammaire générale et raisonnée*, p. 5). Cordemoy announces his goal in similar terms (*op. cit.*, Preface): "je fais en ce discours un discernement exact de tout ce qu'elle [la Parole] tient de l'Ame, et de tout ce qu'elle emprunte du Corps." Similarly, Lamy begins his rhetoric by distinguishing between "l'ame des paroles" (that is, "ce qu'elles ont de spirituel," "ce qui nous est particulier"—the capacity of expressing "les idées") from "leur corps" ("ce qu'elles ont de corporel," "ce que les oyseaux qui imitent la voix des hommes ont de commun avec nous," namely, "les sons, qui sont les signes de ses idées").

In short, language has an inner and an outer aspect. A sentence can be studied from the point of view of how it expresses a thought or from the point of view of its physical shape, that is, from the point of view of either semantic interpretation or phonetic interpretation.

Using some recent terminology, we can distinguish the "deep structure" of a sentence from its "surface structure." The former is the underlying abstract structure that determines its semantic interpretation; the latter, the superficial organization of units which determines the phonetic interpretation and which relates to the physical form of the actual utterance, to its perceived or intended form. In these terms, we can formulate a second fundamental conclusion of Cartesian linguistics, namely, that deep and surface structures need not be identical. The underlying organization of a sentence relevant to semantic interpretation is not necessarily revealed by the actual arrangement and phrasing of its given components.

This point is brought out with particular clarity in the Port-Royal *Grammar*, in which a Cartesian approach to language is developed, for the first time, with considerable insight and subtlety.[67] The principal form of thought (but not the only one —cf. p. 41, below) is the judgment, in which something is affirmed of something else. Its linguistic expression is the proposition, the two terms of which are the "*sujet*, qui est ce dont on affirme" and the "*attribut*, qui est ce qu'on affirme" (p. 29). The subject and the attribute may be *simple*, as in *la terre est ronde*, or *complex* ("composé"), as in *un habile Magistrat est un homme utile à la République* or *Dieu invisible a créé le monde visible*. Furthermore, in such cases as these, the complex subject and the complex attribute

enferment, au moins dans nostre esprit, plusieurs jugemens dont on peut faire autant de propositions: Comme quand je dis, *Dieu invisible a créé le monde visible,* il se passe trois jugemens dans mon esprit renfermez dans cette proposition. Car je juge premierement que *Dieu est invisible.* 2.Qu'*il a créé le monde.* 3. Que *le monde est visible.* Et de ces trois propositions, la seconde est la principale et l'essentielle de la proposition. Mais la première et la troisième ne sont qu'incidentes, et ne font que partie de la principale, dont la première en compose le sujet, et la seconde l'attribut (p. 68).

In other words, the deep structure underlying the proposition *Dieu invisible a créé le monde visible* consists of three abstract propositions, each expressing a certain simple judgment, although its surface form expresses only the subject-attribute structure. Of course, this deep structure is implicit only; it is not expressed but is only represented in the mind:

> or, ces propositions incidentes sont souvent dans nostre esprit, sans estre exprimées par des paroles, comme dans l'exemple proposée (viz., *Dieu invisible a créé le monde visible*; p. 68).

It is sometimes possible to express the deep structure in a more explicit way, in the surface form, "comme quand je reduis le mesme exemple à ces termes: *Dieu QUI est invisible a créé le monde QUI est visible*" (pp. 68–69). But it constitutes an underlying mental reality—a mental accompaniment to the utterance—whether or not the surface form of the utterance that is produced corresponds to it in a simple, point-by-point manner.

In general, constructions of a noun with a noun in apposition, an adjective, or a participle are based on a deep structure containing a relative clause: ". . . toutes ces façons de parler enferment le relatif dans le sens, et se peuvent resoudre par le relatif" (p. 69). The same deep structure may be realized differently in different languages, as when Latin has *video canem currentem*, and French *je voy un chien qui court* (pp. 69–70). The position of the relative pronoun in the "proposition incidente" is determined by a rule that converts deep structure to surface structure. We see this, for example, in such phrases as *Dieu que j'ayme, Dieu par qui le monde a esté créé*. In such cases,

> on met tousjours le relatif à la tête de la proposition (quoy que selon le sens il ne deust estre qu'à la fin) si ce n'est qu'il soit gouverné par une preposition [in which case] la preposition precede au moins ordinairement (p. 71).

In the case of each of the sentences just discussed, the deep structure consists of a system of propositions, and it does not receive a direct, point-by-point expression in the actual physical object that is produced. To form an actual sentence from such an underlying system of elementary propositions, we apply certain rules (in modern terms, grammatical transformations). In these examples, we apply the rule preposing the relative pronoun that takes the place of the noun of the incident proposition (along with the preposition that precedes it, if there is one). We may then, optionally, go on to delete the relative pronoun, at the same time deleting the copula (as in *Dieu invisible*) or changing the form of the verb (as in *canis currens*). Finally, we must, in certain cases, interchange the order of the noun and the adjective (as in *un habile magistrat*).[68]

The deep structure that expresses the meaning is common to all languages, so it is claimed, being a simple reflection of the forms of thought. The transformational rules that convert deep to surface structure may differ from language to language. The surface structure resulting from these transformations does not directly express the meaning relations of the words, of course, except in the simplest cases. It is the deep structure underlying the actual utterance, a structure that is purely mental, that conveys the semantic content of the sentence. This deep structure is, nevertheless, related to actual sentences in that each of its component abstract propositions (in the cases just discussed) could be directly realized as a simple propositional judgment.

The theory of essential and incident propositions, as constituent elements of deep structure, is extended in the Port-Royal *Logic*[69] with a more detailed analysis of relative clauses. There, a distinction is developed between *explicative* (nonrestrictive or appositive) and *determinative* (restrictive) relative clauses. The distinction is based on a prior analysis of the "comprehension" and "extension" of "universal ideas,"[70] in modern terms, an analysis of meaning and reference. The comprehension of an idea is the set of essential attributes that define it, together with whatever can be deduced from them; its extension is the set of objects that it denotes:

> The comprehension of an idea is the constituent parts which make up the idea, none of which can be removed without destroying the idea. For example, the idea of a triangle is made up of the idea of having three sides, the idea of having three angles, and the idea of having angles whose sum is equal to two right angles, and so on.
>
> The extension of an idea is the objects to which the word expressing the idea can be applied. The objects which belong to the extension of an idea are called the inferiors of that idea, which with respect to them is called the superior. Thus, the general idea of triangle has in its extension triangles of all kinds whatsoever (p. 51).

In terms of these notions, we can distinguish such "explications" as *Paris, which is the largest city in Europe* and *man, who is mortal* from "determinations" such as *transparent bodies, wise men* or *a body which is transparent, men who are pious* (pp. 59–60, 118):

> A complex expression is a mere *explication* if either (1) the idea expressed by the complex expression is already contained in the comprehension of the idea expressed by the principal word of the complex expression, or (2) the idea expressed by the complex expression is the idea of some accidental characteristic of all the inferiors of an idea expressed by the principal word (pp. 59–60).
>
> A complex expression is a *determination* if the extension of the idea expressed by the complex term is less than the extension of the idea expressed by the principal word (p. 60).

In the case of an explicative relative clause, the underlying deep structure actually implies the judgment expressed by this clause, when its relative pronoun is replaced by its antecedent. For example, the sentence *men, who were created to know and love God, . . .* implies that men were created to know and love God. Thus an explicative relative clause has the essential properties of conjunction. But in the case of a restrictive relative clause (a determination), this is obviously not true. Thus in saying *men who are pious are charitable*, we do not affirm either that men are pious or that men are charitable. In stating this proposition,

> we form a complex idea by joining together two simple ideas—the idea of man and the idea of piety—and we judge that the attribute of being charitable is part of this complex idea. Thus the subordinate clause asserts nothing more than that the idea of piety is not incompatible with the idea of man. Having made this judgment we then consider what idea can be affirmed of this complex idea of pious man (p. 119).

Similarly, consider the expression *The doctrine which identifies the sovereign good with the sensual pleasure of the body, which was taught by Epicurus, is unworthy of a philosopher.*[71] This contains the subject *The doctrine which . . . taught by Epicurus* and the predicate *unworthy of a philosopher*. The subject is complex, containing the restrictive relative clause *which identifies the sovereign good with the sensual pleasure of the body* and the explicative relative clause *which was taught by Epicurus*. The relative pronoun in the latter has as its antecedent the complex expression *the doctrine which identifies the sovereign good with the sensual pleasure of the body*. Since the clause *which was taught by Epicurus* is explicative, the original sentence does imply that the doctrine in question was taught by Epicurus. But the relative pronoun of the restrictive clause cannot be replaced by its antecedent, *the doctrine*, to form an assertion implied by the full sentence. Once again, the complex phrase containing the restrictive relative clause and its antecedent expresses a single complex idea formed from the two ideas of a doctrine and of identifying the sovereign good with the sensual pleasure of the body. All this information must be represented in the deep structure of the original sentence, according to the Port-Royal theory, and the semantic interpretation of this sentence must proceed in the manner just indicated, utilizing this information (pp. 119–120).

A restrictive relative clause is based on a proposition, according to the Port-Royal theory, even though this proposition is not affirmed when the relative clause is used in a complex expression. What is affirmed in an expression such as *men who are pious*, as noted above, is no more than the compatibility of the constituent ideas. Hence in the expression *minds which are square are more solid than those which are round*, we may correctly say that the relative clause is "false," in a certain sense, since "the idea of being square" is not compatible with "the idea of mind understood as the principle of thought" (p. 124).

Thus sentences containing explicative as well as restrictive relative clauses are based on systems of propositions (that is, abstract objects constituting the meanings of sentences);[72] but the manner of interconnection is different in the case of an explicative clause, in which the underlying judgment is actually affirmed, and a determinative clause, in which the proposition formed by replacing the relative pronoun by its antecedent is not affirmed but rather constitutes a single complex idea together with this noun.

These observations are surely correct, in essence, and must be accommodated in any syntactic theory that attempts to make the notion "deep structure" precise and to formulate and investigate the principles that relate deep structure to surface organization. In short, these observations must be accommodated in some fashion in any theory of transformational generative grammar. Such a theory is concerned precisely with the rules that specify deep structures and relate them to surface structures and with the rules of semantic and phonological interpretation that apply to deep and surface structures respectively. It is, in other words, in large measure an elaboration and formalization of notions that are implicit and in part expressly formulated in such passages as those just discussed. In many respects, it seems to me quite accurate, then, to regard the theory of transformational generative grammar, as it is developing in current work, as essentially a modern and more explicit version of the Port-Royal theory.

The relative pronoun that occurs in the surface form does not always have the dual function of standing for a noun and connecting propositions, in the Port-Royal theory. It may be "depoüillé de la nature de pronom" and may thus serve only the latter role. For example, in such sentences as *je suppose que vous serez sage* and *je vous dis que vous avez tort,* we find that, in the deep structure, "ces propositions, *vous serez sage, vous avez tort,* ne font que partie des propositions entières: *je suppose,* etc., *je vous dis,* etc." (*Grammaire,* p. 73).[73]

The *Grammar* goes on to argue that infinitival constructions play the same role in the verbal system that relative clauses play in the nominal system, providing a means for extending the verbal system through the incorporation of whole propositions: "l'Infinitif est entre les autres manières du Verbe, ce qu'est le Relatif entre les autres pronoms" (pp. 111–112); like the relative pronoun, "l'Infinitif a pardessus l'affirmation du Verbe ce pouvoir de joindre la proposition où il est à un autre" (p. 112). Thus the meaning of *scio malum esse fugiendum* is conveyed by a deep structure based on the two propositions expressed by the sentences *scio* and *malum est fugiendum.* The transformational rule (in modern terms) that forms the surface structure of the sentence replaces *est* by *esse,* just as the transformations that form such sentences as *Dieu (qui est) invisible a créé le monde (qui est) visible* perform various operations of substitution, reordering, and deletion on the underlying systems of propositions. "Et de là est venu qu'en François nous rendons presque tousiours l'infinitif par l'indicatif du Verbe, et la particule *que. Je scay que le mal est a fuir . . .*" (p. 112). In this case, the identity of deep structure in Latin and French may be somewhat obscured by the fact that the two languages use slightly different transformational operations to derive the surface forms.

The *Grammar* goes on to point out that indirect discourse can be analyzed in a similar way.[74] If the underlying embedded proposition is interrogative, it is the particle *si* rather than *que* that is introduced by the transformational rule, as in *on m'a demandé si je pouvois faire cela*, where the "discours qu'on rapport" is *Pouvez-vous faire cela?* Sometimes, in fact, no particle need be added, a change of person being sufficient, as in *Il m'a demandé: Qui estes-vous?* as compared with *Il m'a demandé; qui j'estois* (p. 113).

Summarizing the Port-Royal theory in its major outlines, a sentence has an inner mental aspect (a deep structure that conveys its meaning) and an outer, physical aspect as a sound sequence. Its surface analysis into phrases may not indicate the significant connections of the deep structure by any formal mark or by the actual arrangement of words. The deep structure is, however, represented in the mind as the physical utterance is produced. The deep structure consists of a system of propositions, organized in various ways. The elementary propositions that constitute the deep structure are of the subject-predicate form, with simple subjects and predicates (i.e., categories instead of more complex phrases). Many of these elementary objects can be independently realized as sentences. It is not true, in general, that the elementary judgments constituting the deep structure are affirmed when the sentence that it underlies is produced; explicative and determinative relatives, for example, differ in this respect. To actually produce a sentence from the deep structure that conveys the thought that it expresses, it is necessary to apply rules of transformation that rearrange, replace, or delete items of the sentence. Some of these are obligatory, further ones optional. Thus *Dieu qui est invisible a créé le monde qui est visible* is distinguished from its paraphrase, *Dieu invisible a créé le monde visible*, by an optional deletion operation, but the transformation that substitutes a relative pronoun for the noun and then preposes the pronoun is obligatory.

This account covers only the sentences based exclusively on judgments. But these, although the principal form of thought, do not exhaust the "operations de nostre esprit," and "on y doit encore rapporter les conjonctions, disjonctions, et autres semblables operations de nostre esprit; et tous les autres mouvemens de nostre ame; comme les desirs, le commandment, l'interrogation, etc." (p. 29). In part, these other "forms of thought" are signified by special particles such as *non, vel, si, ergo,* etc. (pp. 137–138). But with respect to these sentence types as well, an identity of deep structure may be masked through divergence of the transformational means whereby actual sentences are formed, corresponding to intended meanings. A case in point is interrogation. In Latin, the interrogative particle *ne* "n'a point d'objet hors de nostre esprit, mais marque seulement le mouvement de nostre ame, par lequel nous souhaittons de sçavoir une chose" (p. 138). As for the interrogative pronoun, "ce n'est autre chose qu'un pronom, auquel est jointe la signification de *ne,* c'est a dire, qui outre qu'il tient la place d'un nom, comme les autres pronoms, marque plus ce mouvement de nostre ame, qui veut sçavoir une chose, et qui demande d'en estre instruitte" (p. 138). But this "mouvement de l'ame" can be signified in various ways other than by the addition of a particle, for example, by vocal inflection or inversion of word order, as in French, where the pronominal subject is "transported" to the position following the person marker of the verb (preserving the agreement of the underlying form). These are all devices for realizing the same deep structure (pp. 138–139).

Notice that the theory of deep and surface structure as developed in the Port-Royal linguistic studies implicitly contains recursive devices and thus provides for infinite use of the finite means that it disposes, as any adequate theory of language must. We see, moreover, that, in the examples given, the recursive devices meet certain formal conditions that have no a priori necessity. In both the trivial cases (e.g., conjunction, disjunction, etc.) and the more interesting ones discussed in connection with relatives and infinitives, the only method for extending deep structures is by adding full propositions of a basic subject-

predicate form. The transformational rules of deletion, rearrangement, etc., do not play a role in the creation of new structures.
The extent to which the Port-Royal grammarians may have been
aware of or interested in these properties of their theory is, of
course, an open question.

In modern terms, we may formalize this view by describing
the syntax of a language in terms of two systems of rules: a *base
system* that generates deep structures and a *transformational system* that maps these into surface structures. The base system consists of rules that generate the underlying grammatical relations
with an abstract order (the rewriting rules of a phrase-structure
grammar); the transformational system consists of rules of deletion, rearrangement, adjunction, and so on. The base rules allow
for the introduction of new propositions (that is, there are rewriting rules of the form: $A \rightarrow \ldots S \ldots$, where S is the initial
symbol of the phrase-structure grammar that constitutes the
base); there are no other recursive devices. Among the transformations are those which form questions, imperatives, etc.,
when the deep structure so indicates (i.e., when the deep structure represents the corresponding "mental act" in an appropriate
notation).[75]

The Port-Royal grammar is apparently the first to develop the
notion of phrase structure in any fairly clear way.[76] It is interesting, therefore, to notice that it also states quite clearly the
inadequacy of phrase-structure description for the representation
of syntactic structure and that it hints at a form of transformational grammar in many respects akin to that which is being
actively studied today.

Turning from the general conception of grammatical structure
to specific cases of grammatical analysis, we find many other
attempts in the Port-Royal grammar to develop the theory of
deep and surface structure. Thus adverbs are analyzed as (for the
most part) arising from "le desir que les hommes ont d'abreger
le discours," thus as being elliptical forms of preposition-noun
constructions, for example, *sapienter* for *cum sapentia* or *hodie*

for *in hoc die* (p. 88). Similarly, verbs are analyzed as containing implicitly an underlying copula that expresses affirmation; thus, once again, as arising from the desire to abbreviate the actual expression of thought. The verb, then, is *"un mot dont le principal usage*[77] *est de signifier l'affimation:* c'est à dire, de marquer que le discours où ce mot est employé, est le discours d'un homme qui ne conçoit pas seulement les choses, mais qui en juge et qui les affirme" (p. 90). To use a verb, then, is to perform the act of affirming, not simply to refer to affirmation, as an "objet de nostre pensée," as in the use of "quelques noms qui signifient aussi l'affirmation; comme *affirmans, affirmatio*" (p. 90). Thus the sentence *Petrus vivit* or *Pierre vit* has the meaning of *Pierre est vivant* (p. 91), and, in the sentence *Petrus affirmat,* "*affirmat* est la mesme chose que *est affirmans*" (p. 98). It follows, then, that in the sentence *affirmo* (in which subject, copula, and attribute are all abbreviated in a single word), two affirmations are expressed: one, regarding the act of the speaker in affirming, the other, the affirmation that he attributes (to himself, in this case). Similarly, "le verbe nego . . . contient une affirmation et une negation" (p. 98).[78]

Formulating these observations in the framework outlined above, what the Port-Royal grammarians are maintaining is that the deep structure underlying a sentence such as *Peter lives* or *God loves mankind* (*Logic*, p. 108) contains a copula, expressing the affirmation, and a predicate (*living, loving mankind*) attributed to the subject of the proposition. Verbs constitute a subcategory of predicates; they are subject to a transformation that causes them to coalesce with the copula into a single word.

The analysis of verbs is extended in the *Logic*, where it is maintained (p. 117) that, despite surface appearances, a sentence with a transitive verb and its object "expresses a complex proposition and in one sense two propositions." Thus we can contradict the sentence *Brutus killed a tyrant* by saying that Brutus did not kill anyone or that the person whom Brutus killed was not a tyrant. It follows that the sentence expresses the proposition that

Brutus killed someone who was a tyrant, and the deep structure must reflect this fact. It seems that this analysis would also apply, in the view of the *Logic*, if the object is a singular term; e.g., *Brutus killed Caesar*.

This analysis plays a role in the theory of reasoning developed later on in the *Logic*. It is used to develop what is in effect a partial theory of relations, permitting the theory of the syllogism to be extended to arguments to which it would otherwise not apply. Thus it is pointed out (pp. 206–207) that the inference from *The divine law commands us to honor kings* and *Louis XIV is a king* to *the divine law commands us to honor Louis XIV* is obviously valid, though it does not exemplify any valid figure as it stands, superficially. By regarding *kings* as "the subject of a sentence contained implicitly in the original sentence," using the passive transformation[79] and otherwise decomposing the original sentence into its underlying propositional constituents, we can finally reduce the argument to the valid figure *Barbara*.

Reduction of sentences to underlying deep structure is resorted to elsewhere in the *Logic*, for the same purpose. For example, Arnauld observes (p. 208) that the sentence *There are few pastors nowadays ready to give their lives for their sheep*, though superficially affirmative in form, actually "contains implicitly the negative sentence *Many pastors nowadays are not ready to give their lives for their sheep*." In general, he points out repeatedly that what is affirmative or negative "in appearance" may or may not be in meaning, that is, in deep structure. In short, the real "logical form" of a sentence may be quite different from its surface grammatical form.[80]

The identity of deep structure underlying a variety of surface forms in different languages is frequently stressed, throughout this period, in connection with the problem of how the significant semantic connections among the elements of speech are expressed. Chapter VI of the Port-Royal *Grammar* considers the expression of these relations in case systems, as in the classical languages, or by internal modification, as in the construct state in Hebrew, or by particles, as in the vernacular languages, or simply by a fixed word order,[81] as in the case of the subject-verb and verb-object relations in French. These are regarded as all being manifestations of an underlying structure common to all these languages and mirroring the structure of thought. Similarly, Lamy comments in his rhetoric on the diverse means used by various languages to express the "rapports, et la suite et la liaison de toutes les idées que la consideration de ces choses excite dans notre esprit" (*op. cit.*, pp. 10–11). The encyclopedist Du Marsais also stresses the fact that case systems express relations among the elements of discourse that are, in other languages, expressed by word order or specific particles, and he points out the correlation between freedom to transpose and wealth of inflection.[82]

Notice that what is assumed is the existence of a uniform set of relations into which words can enter, in any language, these corresponding to the exigencies of thought. The philosophical grammarians do not try to show that all languages literally have case systems, that they use inflectional devices to express these relations. On the contrary, they repeatedly stress that a case system is only one device for expressing these relations. Occasionally, they point out that case names can be assigned to these relations as a pedagogic device; they also argue that considerations of simplicity sometimes may lead to a distinction of cases even where there is no difference in form. The fact that French has no case system is in fact noted in the earliest grammars. Cf. Sahlin, p. 212.

It is important to realize that the use of the names of classical cases for languages with no inflections implies only a belief in the uniformity of the grammatical relations involved, a belief that deep structures are fundamentally the same across languages, although the means for their expression may be quite diverse. This claim is not obviously true—it is, in other words, a nontrivial hypothesis. So far as I know, however, modern linguistics offers no data that challenges it in any serious way.[83]

As noted above, the Port-Royal *Grammar* holds that for the

most part, adverbs do not, properly speaking, constitute a category of deep structure but function only "pour signifier en un seul mot, ce qu'on ne pourroit marquer que par une preposition et un nom" (p. 88). Later grammarians simply drop the qualification to "most adverbs." Thus for Du Marsais, "ce qui distingue l'adverbe des autres espèces de mots, c'est que l'adverbe vaut autant qu'une préposition et un nom: il a la valeur d'une préposition avec son complément: c'est un mot qui abrège" (p. 660). This is an unqualified characterization, and he goes on to analyze a large class of items in this way—in our paraphrase, as deriving from a deep structure of the form: preposition-complement. This analysis is carried still further by Beauzée.[84] He, incidentally, maintains that, although a "phrase adverbiale" such as *avec sagesse* does not differ from the corresponding adverb *sagement* in its "signification," it may differ in the "idées accessoires" associated with it: "quand il s'agit de mettre un acte en opposition avec l'habitude, l'Adverbe est plus propre à marquer l'habitude, et la phrase adverbiale à indiquer l'acte: et je dirois: *un homme que se conduit* sagement *ne peut pas se promettre que toutes ses actions seront faites* avec sagesse" (p. 342).[85] This distinction is a particular case of "l'eloignement que toutes les langues ont naturellement pour une synonymie entière, qui n'enrichiroit un idiome que de sons inutiles à la justesse et à la clarté de l'expression."

Earlier grammarians provide additional instances of analysis in terms of deep structure, as, for example, when imperatives and interrogatives are analyzed as, in effect, elliptical transforms of underlying expressions with such supplementary terms as *I order you* . . . or *I request*. . . .[86] Thus *venez me trouvez* has the deep structure *je vous ordonne (prie) de me venir trouver; qui a trouvé cela?* has the meaning of *je demande celui qui a trouvé cela;* etc.

Still another example that might be cited is the transformational derivation of expressions with conjoined terms from underlying sentences, in the obvious way; for example, in Beauzée, *op. cit.*, pp. 399f. Beauzée's discussion of conjunctions also provides somewhat more interesting cases, as, for example, when he analyses *comment* as based on an underlying form with *manière* and a relative clause, so that the sentence *je sais comment la chose se passa* has the meaning, *je sais la manière de laquelle manière la chose se passa;* or when he analyzes *la maison dont j'ai fait l'acquisition* as meaning *la maison de laquelle maison j'ai fait l'acquisition.* In this way, the underlying deep structure with its essential and incident propositions is revealed.

An interesting further development, along these lines, is carried out by Du Marsais in his theory of *construction* and *syntax.*[87] He proposes that the term "construction" be applied to "l'arrangement des mots dans le discours," and the term "syntaxe," to the "rapports que les mots ont entre eux." For example, the three sentences *accepi litteras tuas, tuas accepi litteras,* and *litteras accepi tuas* exhibit three different constructions, but they have the same syntax; the relations among the constituent elements are the same in all three cases. "Ainsi, chacun de ces trois arrangemens excite dans l'esprit le même sens, *J'ai reçu votre lettre.*" He goes on to define "syntaxe" as "ce qui fait en chaque langue, que les mots excitent le sens que l'on veut faire naître dans l'esprit de ceux qui savent la langue . . . la partie de la Grammaire qui donne la connoissance des signes établis dans une langue pour exciter un sens dans l'esprit" (pp. 229–231). The syntax of an expression is thus essentially what we have called its deep structure; its construction is what we have called its surface structure.[88]

The general framework within which this distinction is developed is the following. An act of the mind is a single unit. For a child, the "sentiment" that sugar is sweet is at first an unanalyzed, single experience (p. 181); for the adult, the meaning of the sentence *le sucre est doux,* the thought that it expresses, is also a single entity. Language provides an indispensable means for the analysis of these otherwise undifferentiated objects. It provides a

moyen d'habiller, pour ainsi dire, notre pensée, de la rendre sensible, de la diviser, de l'analyser, en un mot, de la rendre telle qu'elle puisse être communiquée aux autres avec plus de précision et de détail.

Ainsi, les pensées particulières sont, pour ainsi dire, chacune un ensemble, un tout que l'usage de la parole divise, analyse et distribue en détail par le moyen des différentes articulations des organes de la parole qui forment les mots (p. 184).

Similarly, the perception of speech is a matter of determining the unified and undifferentiated thought from the succession of words. "[Les mots] concourent ensemble à exciter dans l'esprit de celui qui lit, ou qui écoute, le sens total ou la pensée que nous voulons faire naître" (p. 185). To determine this thought, the mind must first discover the relations among the words of the sentence, that is, its syntax; it must then determine the meaning, given a full account of this deep structure. The method of analysis used by the mind is to bring together those words that are related, thus establishing an "ordre significatif" in which related elements are successive. The actual sentence may, in itself, have this "ordre significatif," in which case it is called a "construction simple (naturelle, nécessaire, significative, énonciative)" (p. 232). Where it does not, this "ordre significatif" must be reconstructed by some procedure of analysis—it must be "rétabli par l'esprit, qui n'entend le sens que par cet ordre" (pp. 191–192). To understand a sentence of Latin, for example, you must reconstruct the "natural order" that the speaker has in his mind (p. 196). You must not only understand the meanings of each word, but, furthermore,

vous n'y comprendriez rien non plus, si par une vue de l'esprit vous ne rapprochiez les mots qui ont relation l'un à l'autre. Ce que vous ne pouvez faire qu'après avoir entendu toute la phrase (pp. 198–199).

In Latin, for example, it is the "terminaisons relatives, qui après que toute la Proposition est finie, nous les [that is, les mots] font regarder selon l'ordre de leurs rapports, et par consequent selon l'ordre de la *construction simple*, *nécessaire* et *significative*" (pp.

241–242). This "construction simple" is an "ordre toujours indiqué, mais rarement observé dans la construction usuelle des langues dont les noms ont des cas" (p. 251). Reduction to the "construction simple" is an essential first step in speech perception:

> Les mots forment un tout qui a des parties: or la perception simple du raport que ces parties ont l'une à l'autre, et qui nous en fait concevoir l'ensemble, nous vient uniquement de la construction simple, qui, énonçant les mots suivant l'ordre successif de leurs raports, nous les présente de la manière la plus propre à nous faire apercevoir ces raports, et à faire naitre la pensée totale (pp. 287–288).

Constructions other than the "constructions simples" (namely, "constructions figurées")

> ne sont entendues, que parce que l'esprit en rectifie l'irrégularité, par le secours des idées accessoires, qui font concevoir ce qu'on lit et ce qu'on entend, comme si le sens étoit énoncé dans l'ordre de la construction simple (p. 292).

In short, in the "construction simple" the relations of "syntaxe" are represented directly in the associations among successive words, and the undifferentiated thought expressed by the sentence is derived directly from this underlying representation, which is regarded, throughout, as common to all languages (and, typically, as corresponding to the usual order of French—cf., e.g., p. 193).

The transformations which form a "construction figurée" effect reordering and ellipsis. The "principe fondamental de toute syntaxe" (p. 218) is that reordering and ellipsis must be recoverable by the mind of the hearer (cf. pp. 202, 210ff., 277); that is, they can be applied only when it is possible to recover uniquely "l'ordre sec et métaphysique" of the "construction simple."[89]

Many examples of reduction to "construction simple" are presented to illustrate this theory.[90] Thus the sentence *qui est-ce qui vous l'a dit?* is reduced to the "construction simple" (*celui ou celle*) *qui vous l'a dit est quelle personne?* (Sahlin, p. 93); the sentence *Aussitôt aimés qu'amoureux, On ne vous force point à répandre des larmes* is reduced to *comme vous êtes aimés aussitôt que vous êtes amoureux, . . .*; the sentence *il vaut mieux être juste, que d'être riche; être raisonable que d'être savant* is reduced to four underlying propositions, two negative, two positive, in the obvious way (Sahlin, p. 109); etc.

A rather different sort of example of the distinction between deep and surface structure is provided by Du Marsais in his analysis (pp. 179–180) of such expressions as *j'ai une idée, j'ai peur, j'ai un doute*, etc. These, he says, should not be interpreted as analogous to the superficially similar expressions *j'ai un livre, j'ai un diamant, j'ai une montre*, in which the nouns are "noms d'objets réels qui existent independamment de notre manière de penser." In contrast, the verb in *j'ai une idée* is "une expression empruntée," produced only "par une imitation." The meaning of *j'ai une idée* is simply *je pense, je conçois de telle ou telle manière.* Thus the grammar gives no license for supposing that such words as *idée, concept, imagination* stand for "objets réels," let alone "êtres sensibles." From this grammatical observation it is only a short step to a criticism of the theory of ideas, in its Cartesian and empiricist forms, as based on a false grammatical analogy. This step is taken by Thomas Reid, shortly after.[91]

As Du Marsais indicates with abundant references, his theory of syntax and construction is foreshadowed in scholastic and renaissance grammar (see note 67). But he follows the Port-Royal grammarians in regarding the theory of deep and surface structure as, in essence, a psychological theory, not merely a means for the elucidation of given forms or for analysis of texts. As indicated above, it plays a role in his hypothetical account of the perception and production of speech, just as, in the Port-Royal *Grammar*, the deep structure is said to be represented "dans l'esprit" as the utterance is heard or produced.

As a final example of the attempt to discover the hidden regularities underlying surface variety, we may mention the analysis of indefinite articles in Chapter VII of the Port-Royal *Grammar*, where it is argued, on grounds of symmetry of patterning, that *de* and *des* play the role of the plural of *un*, as in *Un crime si horrible mérite la mort, des crimes si horribles méritent la mort, de si horribles crimes méritent la mort,* etc. To handle the apparent exception, *il est coupable de crimes horribles (d'horribles crimes)*, they propose the "rule of cacophony" that a *de de* sequence is replaced by *de*. They also note the use of *des* as a realization of the definite article, and other uses of these forms.

Perhaps these comments and examples are sufficient to suggest something of the range and character of the grammatical theories of the "philosophical grammarians." As noted above, their theory of deep and surface structure relates directly to the problem of creativity of language use, discussed in the first part of the present work.

From the standpoint of modern linguistic theory, this attempt to discover and characterize deep structure and to study the transformational rules that relate it to surface form is something of an absurdity;[92] it indicates lack of respect for the "real language" (i.e., the surface form) and lack of concern for "linguistic fact." Such criticism is based on a restriction of the domain of "linguistic fact" to physically identifiable subparts of actual utterances and their formally marked relations.[93] Restricted in this way, linguistics studies the use of language for the expression of thought only incidentally, to the quite limited extent to which deep and surface structure coincide; in particular, it studies "sound-meaning correspondences" only in so far as they are representable in terms of surface structure. From this limitation follows the general disparagement of Cartesian and earlier linguistics,[94] which attempted to give a full account of deep structure even where it is not correlated in strict point-by-point fashion to observable features of speech. These traditional attempts to deal with the organization of semantic content as well as the organization of sound were defective in many ways, but modern critique generally rejects them more for their scope than for their failures.

Description and Explanation in Linguistics

Within the framework of Cartesian linguistics, a descriptive grammar is concerned with both sound and meaning; in our terminology, it assigns to each sentence an abstract deep structure determining its semantic content and a surface structure determining its phonetic form. A complete grammar, then, would consist of a finite system of rules generating this infinite set of paired structures and thus showing how the speaker-hearer can make infinite use of finite means in expressing his "mental acts" and "mental states."

However, Cartesian linguistics was not concerned simply with descriptive grammar, in this sense, but rather with "grammaire générale," that is, with the universal principles of language structure. At the very outset of the work under review, a distinction was made between general and particular grammar. These are characterized by Du Marsais in the following way:

> Il y a dans la grammaire des observations qui conviennent à toutes les langues; ces observations forment ce qu'on apelle la grammaire générale: telles sont les remarques que l'on a faites sur les sons articulés, sur les lettres qui sont les signes de ces sons; sur la nature des mots, et sur les diférentes manières dont ils doivent être ou arangés, ou terminés pour faire un sens. Outre ces observations générales, il y en a qui ne sont propres qu'à une langue particulière; et c'est ce qui forme les grammaires particulières de chaque langue.[95]

Beauzée elaborates the distinction in the following way:

> LA GRAMMAIRE, qui a pour objet l'énonciation de la pensée par le secours de la parole prononcée ou écrite, admet donc deux sortes de principes. Les uns sont d'une vérité immuable et d'un usage universel, ils tiennent à la nature de la pensée même, ils en suivent l'analyse, ils n'en sont que le résultat; les autres n'ont qu'une vérité hypothétique, et dépendante des conventions fortuites, arbitraires et muables, qui ont donné naissance aux différents idiômes. Les

premiers constituent la Grammaire générale, les autres sont l'objet des diverses Grammaires particulières.

LA GRAMMAIRE GÉNÉRALE est donc la science raisonnée des principes immuables et généraux du Langage prononcé ou écrit, dans quelque langue que ce soit.

Une GRAMMAIRE PARTICULIÈRE est l'art d'appliquer aux principes immuables et généraux du Langage prononcé ou écrit les institutions arbitraires et usuelles d'une langue particulière.

La *Grammaire Générale* est une *science*, parce qu'elle n'a pour objet que la spéculation raisonnée des principes immuables et généraux du Langage.

Une *Grammaire particulière* est un *art*, parce qu'elle envisage l'application pratique des institutions arbitraires et usuelles d'une langue particulière aux principes généraux du Langage.

La *science grammaticale* est antérieure à toutes les langues, parce que ses principes ne supposent que la possibilité des langues, qu'ils sont les mêmes que ceux qui dirigent la raison humaine dans ses opérations intellectuelles; en un mot, qu'ils sont d'une vérité eternelle.

L'art grammatical, au contraire, est postérieur aux langues, parce que les usages des langues doivent exister avant qu'on les rapporte artificiellement aux principes généraux du Langage, et que les systèmes analogiques qui forment l'art ne peuvent être que le résultat des observations faites sur les usages préexistants.[96]

In his *Eloge de du Marsais*, D'Alembert gives this account of "philosophical grammar":

La Grammaire est donc l'ouvrage des Philosophes;—L'esprit philosophique seul peut remonter jusqu'aux principes sur lesquels les regles sont établies, . . . Cet esprit apperçoit d'abord, dans la Grammaire de chaque Langue, les principes généraux qui sont communs à toutes les autres, et qui forment la Grammaire générale; il démêle ensuite dans les usages particuliers à chaque Langue, ceux qui peuvent être fondés en raison, d'avec ceux qui ne sont que l'ouvrage du hasard ou de la négligence: il observe l'influence réciproque que les Langues ont eue les unes sur les autres, et les altérations que ce mélange leur a données, sans leur ôter entièrement leur premier caractere: il balance leurs avantages et leurs désavantages mutuels; la différence de leur construction . . . ;

la diversité de leur génie . . .; leur richesse et leur liberté, leur indigence et leur servitude. Le développement de ces différens objets est la vraie Métaphysique de la Grammaire.—Son objet est . . . la marche de l'esprit humain dans la génération de ses idées, et dans l'usage qu'il fait des mots pour transmettre ses pensées aux autres hommes.[97]

The discovery of universal principles would provide a partial explanation for the facts of particular languages, in so far as these could be shown to be simply specific instances of the general features of language structure formulated in the "grammaire générale." Beyond this, the universal features themselves might be explained on the basis of general assumptions about human mental processes or the contingencies of language use (for example, the utility of elliptical transformations). Proceeding in this way, Cartesian linguistics attempts to develop a theory of grammar that is not only "générale" but also "raisonnée."

The linguistics of Port-Royal and its successors developed in part in reaction against the prevailing approaches represented, for example, in such work as Vaugelas's *Remarques sur la langue Françoise* (1647).[98] Vaugelas's goal is simply to describe usage, "que chacun reconnoist pour le Maistre et le souverain des langues vivantes" (Preface). His book is called *Remarques . . .* rather than *Decisions . . .* or *Loix . . .* because he is "un simple tesmoin." He disclaims any intention of explaining the facts of speech or finding general principles that underlie them, just as he generally suggests no modification or "purification" of usage on rational or esthetic grounds. His grammar, then, is neither "raisonnée" nor prescriptive.[99] He is quite aware of the problems of determining actual usage and provides an interesting discussion of "elicitation procedures" (pp. 503f.), in which, among other things, he points out the inadequacy of the kinds of "direct question" tests for grammaticalness that have occasionally been proposed and applied by structural linguists, with predictably inconclusive results. He does not restrict his descriptive comments to surface structure.[100] For example, he points out (pp.

562–563) that one cannot determine from the form of a word whether it has a "signification active," or a "signification passive," or, ambiguously, both. Thus in the sentence *mon estime n'est pas une chose dont vous puissiez tirer grand avantage*, the phrase *mon estime* has the sense *l'estime que je fais de vous*, whereas in the sentence *mon estime ne depend pas de vous*, it means *l'estime que l'on fait* or *l'estime que l'on peut faire de moi*; and the same is true of such words as *aide*, *secours*, and *opinion*. There are other examples of a concern for descriptive adequacy on a broad scale. At the same time, Vaugelas's work foreshadows many of the defects of modern linguistic theory, for example, in his failure to recognize the creative aspect of language use. Thus he regards normal language use as constructed of phrases and sentences that are "authorized by usage," although new words (e.g., *brusqueté*, *pleurement*) can be correctly formed by analogy (pp. 568f.). His view of language structure, in this respect, seems not very different from that of Saussure, Jespersen, Bloomfield, and many others who regard innovation as possible only "by analogy," by substitution of lexical items for items of the same category within fixed frames. (Cf. p. 12.)

The reaction of "philosophical grammar" is not against the descriptivism of Vaugelas and others as such[101] but against the restriction to *pure* descriptivism. The Port-Royal grammar takes it as a general maxim for anyone working on a living language that "les façons de parler qui sont authorisées par un usage général et non contesté, doivent passer pour bonnes, encore qu'elles soient contraires aux regles et à l'analogie de la Langue" (p. 83). Lamy, in his rhetoric, echoes Vaugelas in describing usage as "le maistre et l'arbitre souverain des langues" and in holding that "personne ne luy peut contester cet empire que la nécessité a établi, et que le consentment général des peuples a confirmé" (*op. cit.*, p. 31). Du Marsais insists that "le grammarien philosophe doit raisonner de la langue particulière dont il traite relativement à ce que cette langue est en elle-même, et non par rapport à une autre langue."[102] Philosophical grammar, then, was not characteristically attempting to refine or improve language, but to discover its underlying principles and to explain the particular phenomena that are observed.[103]

The example which, for more than a century, was used to illustrate this difference between descriptive and explanatory grammar was provided by a rule of Vaugelas (pp. 385f.) regarding relative clauses, namely, the rule that a relative clause may not be added to a noun that has no articles or only the "article indefini" *de*. Thus one cannot say *il a fait cela par avarice, qui est capable de tout* or *il a fait cela par avarice, dont la soif ne se peut esteindre*. Similarly, one cannot say *il a esté blessé d'un coup de fleche, qui estoit empoisonnée* (p. 385), although it is correct to say *il a esté blessé de la fleche, qui estoit empoisonnée* or *il a esté blessé d'une fleche qui estoit empoisonnée*.

In Chapter IX, the Port-Royal *Grammar* first notes a variety of exceptions to this rule and then proposes a general explanatory principle to account both for the examples that fall under the rule of Vaugelas and for the exceptions to his rule.[104] The explanation is, once again, based on the distinction between meaning and reference. In the case of a "nom commun," the "signification" is fixed (except for ambiguity or metaphor), but the "estendue" varies, depending on the noun phrase in which the noun appears. A particular occurrence of a noun is called "indéterminé," "lors qu'il n'y a rien qui marque s'il doit estre pris generalement ou particulierement, et estant pris particulierement, si c'est pour un particulier certain ou incertain" (p. 77). Otherwise, it is "déterminé." Vaugelas's rule is now restated in terms of "determination": "Dans l'usage present de nostre langue, on ne doit point mettre de *qui* apres un nom commun, s'il n'est déterminé par un article, ou par quelque autre chose qui ne le détermine pas moins que feroit un article" (p. 77). A detailed analysis follows, attempting to show that the apparent counterexamples involve occurrences of nouns that are "determined" by some feature other than the article. In part, the analysis is based on assumptions about deep structure that are not without interest in themselves. The rule is also discussed by Du Marsais, Beauzée, and others at some length. We need not go into the details here. The point, in the present context, is that this was taken as a paradigm example of the necessity for supplementing descriptive statements with a rational explanation, if linguistics was to go beyond compilation of facts to true "science"—in the terminology of the day, if grammar was to become "philosophical."

In connection with the rule of Vaugelas and several other cases, the explanations that are proposed, in universal grammar, have some substance and linguistic content. All too often, however, they are quite empty, and invoke assumptions about underlying mental reality in a quite mechanical and unrevealing way. In fact, it seems to me that in general the modern critique of "philosophical grammar" is quite misplaced. The error of this position is generally taken to be its excessive rationality and a priorism and its disregard for linguistic fact. But a more cogent criticism is that the tradition of philosophical grammar is too limited to mere description of fact—that it is insufficiently "raisonnée"; that is, it seems to me that the faults (or limitations) of this work are just the opposite of those which have been attributed to it by modern critics. The philosophical grammarians considered a wide realm of particular examples; they tried to show, for each example, what was the deep structure that underlies its surface form and expresses the relations among elements that determine its meaning. To this extent, their work is purely descriptive (just as modern linguistics is purely descriptive in pursuit of its more restricted goal of identifying the units that constitute the surface structure of particular utterances, their arrangement into phrases, and their formally marked relations). Reading this work, one is constantly struck by the *ad hoc* character of the analysis, even where it seems factually correct. A deep structure is proposed that does convey the semantic content, but the basis for its selection (beyond mere factual correctness) is generally unformulated. What is missing is a theory of linguistic structure that is articulated with sufficient precision and is sufficiently rich to bear the burden of justification. Although the examples of deep structure that are given in abundance often seem quite plausible, they are unsatisfying, just as modern linguistic descriptions, though often quite plausible in their analysis of particular utterances into phonemes, morphemes, words, and phrases, remain unsatisfying, and for the same reason. In neither case do we have an underlying hypothesis as to the general nature of language that is sufficiently strong as to indicate why just these and not other descriptions are selected by the child acquiring the language or the linguist describing it, on the basis of the data available to them.[105]

What is more, there is little recognition in philosophical grammar of the intricacy of the mechanisms that relate deep to surface structure, and, beyond the general outlines sketched above, there is no detailed investigation of the character of the rules that appear in grammars or the formal conditions that they satisfy. Concomitantly, no clear distinction is made between the abstract structure underlying a sentence and the sentence itself. It is, by and large, assumed that the deep structure consists of actual sentences in a simpler or more natural organization and that the rules of inversion, ellipsis, and so on, that form the full range of actual sentences simply operate on these already formed simple sentences. This point of view is explicit, for example, in Du Marsais's theory of syntax and construction, and it is undoubtedly the general view throughout.[106] The totally unwarranted assumption that a deep structure is nothing other than an arrangement of simple sentences can be traced to the Cartesian postulate that, quite generally, the principles that determine the nature of thought and perception must be accessible to introspection and can be brought to consciousness, with care and attention.

Despite these shortcomings, the insights into the organization of grammar that were achieved in Cartesian linguistics remain quite impressive, and a careful study of this work can hardly fail to prove rewarding to a linguist who approaches it without prejudice or preconceptions as to the a priori limitations on permitted linguistic investigation. Beyond these achievements, the universal grammarians of the seventeenth and eighteenth centuries have made a contribution of lasting value by the very fact that they posed so clearly the problem of changing the orientation of linguistics from "natural history" to "natural philosophy" and by stressing the importance of the search for universal principles and for rational explanation of linguistic fact, if progress is to be made toward this goal.

Acquisition and Use of Language

We have so far extracted from "Cartesian linguistics" certain characteristic and quite important doctrines regarding the nature of language and have, quite sketchily, traced their development during the period from Descartes to Humboldt. As a by-product of this study of *langue*, and against the background of rationalist theory of mind, certain views emerged as to how language is acquired and used. After a long interlude, these views are once again beginning to receive the attention that they deserve, although their appearance (like the reappearance of the central ideas of transformational grammar) was, in fact, a largely independent development.

The central doctrine of Cartesian linguistics is that the general features of grammatical structure are common to all languages and reflect certain fundamental properties of the mind. It is this assumption which led the philosophical grammarians to concentrate on *grammaire générale* rather than *grammaire particulière* and which expresses itself in Humboldt's belief that deep analysis will show a common "form of language" underlying national and individual variety.[107] There are, then, certain language universals that set limits to the variety of human language.[108] The study of the universal conditions that prescribe the form of any human language is "grammaire générale." Such universal conditions are not learned; rather, they provide the organizing principles that make language learning possible, that must exist if data is to lead to knowledge. By attributing such principles to the mind, as an innate property, it becomes possible to account for the quite obvious fact that the speaker of a language knows a great deal that he has not learned.

In approaching the question of language acquisition and linguistic universals in this way, Cartesian linguistics reflects the concern of seventeenth-century rationalistic psychology with the contribution of the mind to human knowledge. Perhaps the earliest exposition of what was to become a major theme, throughout most of this century, is Herbert of Cherbury's *De Veritate* (1624),[109] in which he develops the view that there are certain "principles or notions implanted in the mind" that "we bring to objects from ourselves . . . [as] . . . a direct gift of Nature, a precept of natural instinct" (p. 133). Although these Common Notions "are stimulated by objects," nevertheless, "no one, however wild his views, imagines that they are conveyed by objects themselves" (p. 126). Rather, they are essential to the identification of objects and the understanding of their properties and relations. Although the "intellectual truths" comprised among the Common Notions "seem to vanish in the absence of objects, yet they cannot be wholly passive and idle seeing that they are essential to objects and objects to them . . . It is only with their aid that the intellect, whether in familiar or new types of things, can be led to decide whether our subjective faculties have accurate knowledge of the facts" (p. 105). By application of these intellectual truths, which are "imprinted on the soul by the dictates of Nature itself," we can compare and combine individual sensations and interpret experience in terms of objects, their properties, and the events in which they participate. Evidently, these interpretive principles cannot be learned from experience in their entirety, and they may be independent of experience altogether. According to Herbert:

> [They] are so far from being drawn from experience or
> observation that, without several of them, or at least one of them,

we could have no experience at all nor be capable of observations. For if it had not been written in our soul that we should examine into the nature of things (and we do not derive this command from objects), and if we had not been endowed with Common Notions, to that end, we should never come to distinguish between things, or to grasp any general nature. Vacant forms, prodigies, and fearful images would pass meaninglessly and even dangerously before our minds, unless there existed within us, in the shape of notions imprinted in the mind, that analogous faculty by which we distinguish good from evil. From where else could we have received knowledge? In consequence, anyone who considers to what extent objects in their external relationship contribute to their correct perception; who seeks to estimate what is contributed by us, or to discover what is due to alien or accidental sources, or again to innate influences, or to factors arising from nature, will be led to refer to these principles. We listen to the voice of nature not only in our choice between what is good and evil, beneficial and harmful, but also in that external correspondence by which we distinguish truth from falsehood, we possess hidden faculties which when stimulated by objects quickly respond to them (pp. 105–106).

It is only by the use of these "inborn capacities or Common Notions" that the intellect can determine "whether our subjective faculties have exercised their perceptions well or ill" (p. 87). This "natural instinct" thus instructs us in the nature, manner, and scope of what is to be heard, hoped for, or desired" (p. 132).

Care must be taken in determining what are the Common Notions, the innate organizing principles and concepts that make experience possible. For Herbert, the "chief criterion of Natural Instinct" is "universal consent" (p. 139). But two qualifications are necessary. First, what is referred to is universal consent among "normal men" (p. 105). That is, we must put aside "persons who are out of their minds or mentally incapable" (p. 139) and those who are "headstrong, foolish, weak-minded and imprudent" (p. 125). And although these faculties "may not ever be entirely absent," and "even in madmen, drunkards, and infants extraordinary internal powers may be detected which minister to their safety" (p. 125), still we can expect to find universal consent to

Common Notions only among the normal, rational, and clear-headed. Second, appropriate experience is necessary to elicit or activate these innate principles; "it is the law or destiny of Common Notions and indeed of the other forms of knowledge to be inactive unless objects stimulate them" (p. 120). In this respect, the common notions are like the faculties of seeing, hearing, loving, hoping, etc., with which we are born and which "remain latent when their corresponding objects are not present, and even disappear and give no sign of their existence" (p. 132). But this fact must not blind us to the realization that "the Common Notions must be deemed not so much the outcome of experience as principles without which we should have no experience at all" and to the absurdity of the theory that "our mind is a clean sheet, as though we obtained our capacity for dealing with objects from objects themselves" (p. 132).

The common notions are "all intimately connected" and can be arranged into a system (p. 120); and although "an infinite number of faculties may be awakened in response to an infinite number of new objects, all the Common Notions which embrace this order of facts may be comprehended in a few propositions" (p. 106). This system of common notions is not to be identified with "reason." It simply forms "that part of knowledge with which we were endowed in the primeval plan of Nature," and it is important to bear in mind that "it is the nature of natural instinct to fulfil itself irrationally, that is to say, without foresight." On the other hand, "reason is the process of applying Common Notions as far as it can" (pp. 120–121).

In focusing attention on the innate interpretive principles that are a precondition for experience and knowledge and in emphasizing that these are implicit and may require external stimulation in order to become active or available to introspection, Herbert expressed much of the psychological theory that underlies Cartesian linguistics, just as he emphasized those aspects of cognition that were developed by Descartes and, later, by the English Platonists, Leibniz and Kant.[110]

The psychology that develops in this way is a kind of Platonism without preexistence. Leibniz makes this explicit in many places. Thus he holds that "nothing can be taught us of which we have not already in our minds the idea," and he recalls Plato's "experiment" with the slave boy in the *Meno* as proving that "the soul virtually knows those things [i.e., truths of geometry, in this case], and needs only to be reminded (animadverted) to recognize the truths. Consequently, it possesses at least the idea upon which these truths depend. We may say even that it already possesses those truths, if we consider them as the relations of the ideas" (§26).[111]

Of course, what is latent in the mind in this sense may often require appropriate external stimulation before it becomes active, and many of the innate principles that determine the nature of thought and experience may well be applied quite unconsciously. This Leibniz emphasizes, in particular, throughout his *Nouveaux Essais*.

That the principles of language and natural logic are known unconsciously[112] and that they are in large measure a precondition for language acquisition rather than a matter of "institution" or "training" is the general presupposition of Cartesian linguistics.[113] When Cordemoy, for example, considers language acquisition (*op. cit.*, pp. 40ff.), he discusses the role of instruction and conditioning of a sort, but he also notices that much of what children know is acquired quite apart from any explicit instruction,[114] and he concludes that language learning presupposes possession of "la raison toute entiere; car enfin cette maniere d'apprendre à parler, est l'effet d'un si grand discernement, et d'une raison si parfaite, qu'il n'est pas possible d'en concevoir un plus merveilleux" (p. 59).

Rationalist conclusions reappear with some of the romantics as well. Thus A. W. Schlegel writes that "on pourrait comparer la raison humaine à une matière infiniment combustible, mais qui néanmoins ne s'embrase d'elle même. Il faut qu'une étincelle soit jetée dans l'âme" ("De l'étymologie en général," p. 127). Communication with an already formed intellect is necessary for reason to awaken. But external stimulation is only required to set innate mechanisms to work; it does not determine the form of what is acquired. In fact, it is clear "dass dieses Erlernen [of language] durch Mitteilung schon die Fähigkeit, Sprache zu erfinden, voraussetzt" (*Kunstlehre*, p. 234). In a certain sense, language is innate to man; namely, "im echteren philosophischen Sinne, wo alles, was nach der gewöhnlichen Ansicht dem Menschen angeboren scheint, erst durch seine eigene Tätigkeit hervorgebracht werden muss" (*ibid.*, p. 235). While Schlegel's precise intentions, with many such remarks, might be debated, in Humboldt the Platonism with respect to language acquisition is quite clear. For Humboldt, "die Erlernung ist . . . immer nur Wiedererzeugung" (*op. cit.*, p. 126). Despite superficial appearances, a language "lässt sich . . . nicht eigentlich lehren, sondern nur im Gemüthe wecken; man kann ihr nur den Faden hingeben, an dem sie sich von selbst entwickelt"; thus languages are, in a sense, "Selbstschöpfungen der Individuen" (p. 50):

> Das Sprechenlernen der Kinder ist nicht ein Zumessen von Wörtern, Niederlegen im Gedächtniss, und Wiedernachlallen mit den Lippen, sondern ein Wachsen des Sprachvermögens durch Alter und Übung (p. 21).

> Dass bei den Kindern nicht ein mechanisches Lernen der Sprache, sondern eine Entwickelung der Sprachkraft vorgeht, beweist auch, dass, da den haupsächlichsten menschlichen Kräften ein gewisser Zeitpunkt im Lebensalter zu ihrer Entwicklung angewiesen ist, alle Kinder unter den verschiedenartigsten Umständen ungefähr in demselben, nur innerhalb eines kurzen Zeitraums schwankenden, Alter sprechen und verstehen (p. 72).

In short, language acquisition is a matter of growth and maturation of relatively fixed capacities, under appropriate external conditions. The form of the language that is acquired is largely determined by internal factors; it is because of the fundamental correspondence of all human languages, because of the fact that "der Mensch überall Eins mit dem Menschen ist," that a child can learn any language (pp. 72–73).[115] The functioning of the language capacity is, furthermore, optimal at a certain "critical period" of intellectual development.

It is important to emphasize that seventeenth-century rationalism approaches the problem of learning—in particular, language learning—in a fundamentally nondogmatic fashion. It notes that knowledge arises on the basis of very scattered and inadequate data and that there are uniformities in what is learned that are in no way uniquely determined by the data itself (see note 114). Consequently, these properties are attributed to the mind, as preconditions for experience. This is essentially the line of reasoning that would be taken, today, by a scientist interested in the structure of some device for which he has only input-output data. In contrast, empiricist speculation, particularly in its modern versions, has characteristically adopted certain a priori assumptions regarding the nature of learning (that it must be based on association or reinforcement, or on inductive procedures of an elementary sort—e.g., the taxonomic procedures of modern linguistics, etc.) and has not considered the necessity for checking these assumptions against the observed uniformities of "output"— against what is known or believed after "learning" has taken place. Hence the charge of a priorism or dogmatism often leveled against rationalistic psychology and philosophy of mind seems clearly to be misdirected. For further discussion, see the references of note 110.

The strong assumptions about innate mental structure made by rationalistic psychology and philosophy of mind eliminated the necessity for any sharp distinction between a theory of perception and a theory of learning. In both cases, essentially the same processes are at work; a store of latent principles is brought to the interpretation of the data of sense. There is, to be sure, a difference between the initial "activation" of latent structure and the use of it once it has become readily available for the interpretation (more accurately, the determination) of experience.

The confused ideas that are always latent in the mind may, in other words, become distinct (see note 111), and at this point they can heighten and enhance perception. Thus, for example, a

> skilful and expert limner will observe many elegancies and curiosities of art, and be highly pleased with several strokes and shadows in a picture, where a common eye can discern nothing at all; and a musical artist hearing a consort of exact musicians playing some excellent composure of many parts, will be exceedingly ravished with many harmonical airs and touches, that a vulgar ear will be utterly insensible of (Cudworth, *op. cit.*, p. 446).

It is the "acquired skill" that makes the difference; "the artists of either kind have many inward anticipations of skill and art in their minds" that enable them to interpret the data of sense in a way that goes beyond the "mere noise and sound and clatter" provided by passive sense, just as the informed mind can interpret the "vital machine of the universe" in terms of "interior symmetry and harmony in the relations, proportions, aptitudes and correspondence of things to one another in the great mundane system" (*ibid.*). Similarly, in looking at and "judging of" a picture of a friend, one makes use of a "foreign and adventitious" but preexistent idea (pp. 456–457). Once this distinction between learning and perception has been noted, however, the essential parallel between the cognitive processes that are involved outweighs the relatively superficial differences, from the point of view of this rationalist doctrine. For this reason, it is often unclear whether what is being discussed is the activity of the mind in perception or in acquisition—that is, in selecting an already distinct idea on the occasion of sense, or in making distinct what was before only confused and implicit.

Descartes's theory of cognition is clearly summarized in his *Notes Directed against a Certain Program* (1647; Haldane and Ross, pp. 442–443):

> . . . any man who rightly observes the limitations of the senses, and what precisely it is that can penetrate through this medium to

our faculty of thinking must needs admit that no ideas of things, in the shape in which we envisage them by thought, are presented to us by the senses. So much so that in our ideas there is nothing which was not innate in the mind, or faculty of thinking, except only these circumstances which point to experience—the fact, for instance, that we judge that this or that idea, which we now have present to our thought, is to be referred to a certain extraneous thing, not that these extraneous things transmitted the ideas themselves to our minds through the organs of sense, but because they transmitted something which gave the mind occasion to form these ideas, by means of an innate faculty, at this time rather than at another. For nothing reaches our mind from external objects through the organs of sense beyond certain corporeal movements . . . but even these movements, and the figures which arise from them, are not conceived by us in the shape they assume in the organs of sense . . . Hence it follows that the ideas of the movements and figures are themselves innate in us. So much the more must the ideas of pain, color, sound, and the like be innate, that our mind may, on occasion of certain corporeal movements, envisage these ideas, for they have no likeness to the corporeal movements. Could anything be imagined more preposterous than that all common notions which are inherent in our mind should arise from these movements, and should be incapable of existing without them? I should like *our friend* to instruct me as to what corporeal movement it is which can form in our mind any common notion, e.g., the notion that *things which are equal to the same thing are equal to one another*, or any other he pleases; for all these movements are particular, but notions are universal having no affinity with the movements and no relation to them.

Rather similar ideas are developed at length by Cudworth.[116] He distinguished the essentially passive faculty of sense from the active and innate "cognoscitive powers" whereby men (and men alone) "are enabled to understand or judge of what is received from without by sense." This cognoscitive power is not a mere storehouse of ideas, but "a power of raising intelligible ideas and conceptions of things from within itself" (p. 425). The function of sense is "the offering or presenting of some object to the mind, to give it an occasion to exercise its own activity upon." Thus, for example, when we look into the street and perceive men walking, we are relying, not merely on sense (which shows us at most surfaces—i.e., hats and clothes—and, in fact, not even objects), but on the exercise of the understanding, applied to the data of sense (pp. 409–410).[117] The "intelligible forms by which things are understood or known, are not stamps or impressions passively printed upon the soul from without, but ideas vitally protended or actively exerted from within itself." Thus prior knowledge and set play a large role in determining what we see (e.g., a familiar face in a crowd) (pp. 423–424). It is because we use intellectual ideas in perception "that those knowledges which are more abstract and remote from matter, are more accurate, intelligible and demonstrable,—than those which are conversant about concrete and material things," as Aristotle has observed (p. 427).[118] This claim is illustrated by a discussion of our conceptions of geometrical figures (pp. 455f.). Obviously every sensed triangle is irregular, and if there were a physically perfect one, we could not detect this by sense; "and every irregular and imperfect triangle [is] as perfectly that which it is, as the most perfect triangle." Our judgments regarding external objects in terms of regular figures, our very notion of "regular figure" therefore have their source in the "rule, pattern and exemplar" which are generated by the mind as an "anticipation." The concept of a triangle or of a "regular proportionate and symmetrical figure" is not taught but "springs originally from nature itself," as does, in general, the human concept of "pulchritude and deformity in material objects"; nor can the a priori truths of geometry be derived from sense. And it is only by means of these "inward ideas" produced by its "innate cognoscitive power" that the mind is able to "know and understand all external individual things" (p. 482).

Descartes had discussed the same question in very similar terms, in his *Reply to Objections V*:

> Hence when first in infancy we see a triangular figure depicted on paper, this figure cannot show us how a real triangle ought

to be conceived, in the way in which geometricians consider it, because the true triangle is contained in this figure, just as the statue of Mercury is contained in a rough block of wood. But because we already possess within us the idea of a true triangle, and it can be more easily conceived by our mind than the more complex figure of the triangle drawn on paper, we, therefore, when we see that composite figure, apprehend not it itself, but rather the authentic triangle (Haldane and Ross, *op. cit.*, vol. II, pp. 227–228).

For Cudworth, the interpretation of sensory data in terms of objects and their relations, in terms of cause and effect, the relations of whole and part, symmetry, proportion, the functions served by objects and the characteristic uses to which they are put (in the case of all "things artificial" or "compounded natural things"), moral judgments, etc., is the result of the organizing activity of the mind (pp. 433f.). The same is true of the unity of objects (or, for example, of a melody); sense is like a "narrow telescope" that provides only piecemeal and successive views, but only the mind can give "one comprehensive idea of the whole" with all its parts, relations, proportions, and Gestalt qualities. It is in this sense that we speak of the intelligible idea of an object as not "stamped or impressed upon the soul from without, but upon occasion of the sensible idea excited and exerted from the inward active and comprehensive power of the intellect itself" (p. 439).[119]

Ideas of this sort regarding perception were common in the seventeenth century but were then swept aside by the empiricist current, to be revived again by Kant and the romantics.[120] Consider, for example, Coleridge's remarks on active processes in perception:

Instances in which a knowledge given to the mind quickens and invigorates the faculties by which such knowledge is attainable independently cannot have escaped the most ordinary observer, and this is equally true whether it be faculties of the mind or of the senses. . . . It is indeed wonderful both how small a likeness

will suffice a full apprehension of sound or sight when the
correspondent sound or object is foreknown and foreimagined
and how small a deviation or imperfection will render the whole
confused and indistinguishable or mistaken where no such previous
intimation has been received. Hence all unknown languages appear
to a foreigner to be spoken by the natives with extreme rapidity
and to those who are but beginning to understand it with a
distressing indistinction.[121]

Does nature present objects to us without exciting any act on
our part, does she present them under all circumstances perfect
and as it were ready made? Such may be the notion of the most
unthinking . . . not only must we have some scheme or general
outline of the object to which we could determine to direct our
attention, were it only to have the power of recognizing it. . . .[122]

It is, once again, with Humboldt that these ideas are applied
most clearly to the perception and interpretation of speech. He
argues (*Verschiedenheit*, pp. 70–71) that there is a fundamental
difference between the perception of speech and the perception
of unarticulated sound (cf. note 38). For the latter, "das thierische
Empfindungsvermögen" would suffice. But human speech perception is not merely a matter of "das blosse gegenseitige Her-
vorrufen des Lauts und des angedeuteten Gegenstandes." For one
thing, a word is not "ein Abdruck des Gegenstandes an sich,
sondern des von diesem in der Seele erzeugten Bildes" (p. 74).
But, furthermore, speech perception requires an analysis of the
incoming signal in terms of the underlying elements that function
in the essentially creative act of speech production, and therefore it requires the activation of the generative system that plays
a role in production of speech as well, since it is only in terms of
these fixed rules that the elements and their relations are defined.
The underlying "Gesetze der Erzeugung" must, therefore, function in speech perception. If it were not for its mastery of these,
if it were not for its ability "jene Möglichkeit zur Wirklichkeit
zu bringen," the mind would no more be able to deal with the
mechanisms of articulated speech than a blind man is able to perceive colors. It follows, then, that both the perceptual mechanisms

and the mechanisms of speech production must make use of the underlying system of generative rules. It is because of the virtual identity of this underlying system in speaker and hearer that communication can take place, the sharing of an underlying generative system being traceable, ultimately, to the uniformity of human nature (cf. pp. 64–65 and note 115). In brief,

> Es kann in der Seele nichts, als durch eigne Thätigkeit, vorhanden sein, und Verstehen und Sprechen sind nur verschiedenartige Wirkungen der nämlichen Sprachkraft. Die gemeinsame Rede ist nie mit dem Übergeben eines Stoffes vergleichbar. In dem Verstehenden, wie im Sprechenden, muss derselbe aus der eigenen, inneren Kraft entwickelt werden; und was der erstere empfängt, ist nur die harmonisch stimmende Anregung. . . . Auf diese Weise liegt die Sprache in jedem Menschen in ihrem ganzen Umfange, was aber nichts Anderes bedeutet, als dass jeder ein, durch eine bestimmt modificirte Kraft, anstossend und beschränkend, geregeltes Streben besitzt, die ganze Sprache, wie es äussere oder innere Veranlassung herbeiführt, nach und nach aus sich hervorzubringen und hervorgebracht zu verstehen.
>
> Das Verstehen könnte jedoch nicht, so wie wir es eben gefunden haben, auf innerer Selbstthätigkeit beruhen, und das gemeinschaftliche Sprechen müsste etwas Andres, als bloss gegenseitiges Wecken des Sprachvermögens des Hörenden, sein, wenn nicht in der Verschiedenheit der Einzelnen die, sich nur in abgesonderte Individualitäten spaltende, Einheit der menschlichen Natur läge.

Even in the case of perception of a single word, an underlying system of generative rules must be activated. It would be inaccurate, Humboldt maintains, to suppose that speaker and hearer share a store of clear and totally formed concepts. Rather, the perceived sound incites the mind to generate a corresponding concept by its own means:

> Die Menschen verstehen einander nicht dadurch, dass sie sich Zeichen der Dinge wirklich hingeben, auch nicht dadurch, dass sie sich gegenseitig bestimmen, genau und vollständig denselben Begriff hervorzubringen, sondern dadurch, dass sie gegenseitig in

einander dasselbe Glied der Kette ihrer sinnlichen Vorstellungen und inneren Begriffserzeugungen berühren, dieselbe Taste ihres geistigen Instruments anschlagen, worauf alsdann in jedem entsprechende, nicht aber dieselben Begriffe hervorspringen (p. 213).

In short, speech perception requires internal generation of a representation both of the signal and the associated semantic content.

Contemporary research in perception has returned to the investigation of the role of internally represented schemata or models[123] and has begun to elaborate the somewhat deeper insight that it is not merely a store of schemata that function in perception but rather a system of fixed rules for generating such schemata.[124] In this respect too, it would be quite accurate to describe current work as a continuation of the tradition of Cartesian linguistics and the psychology that underlies it.

Summary

Returning to the remark of Whitehead's that initiated this discussion, it seems that after a long interruption, linguistics and cognitive psychology are now turning their attention to approaches to the study of language structure and mental processes which in part originated and in part were revitalized in the "century of genius" and which were fruitfully developed until well into the nineteenth century. The creative aspect of language use is once again a central concern of linguistics, and the theories of universal grammar that were outlined in the seventeenth and eighteenth centuries have been revived and elaborated in the theory of transformational generative grammar. With this renewal of the study of universal formal conditions on the system of linguistic rules, it becomes possible to take up once again the search for deeper explanations for the phenomena found in particular languages and observed in actual performance. Contemporary work has finally begun to face some simple facts about language that have been long neglected, for example, the fact that the speaker of a language knows a great deal that he has not learned and that his normal linguistic behavior cannot possibly be accounted for in terms of "stimulus control," "conditioning," "generalization and analogy," "patterns" and "habit structures," or "dispositions to respond," in any reasonably clear sense of these much abused terms. As a result, a fresh look has been taken, not only at language structure, but at the preconditions for language acquisition and at the perceptual function of abstract systems of internalized rules. I have tried to indicate, in this summary of Cartesian linguistics and the theory of mind from which it arose, that much of what is coming to light in this work was foreshadowed or even explicitly formulated in earlier and now largely forgotten studies.

It is important to bear in mind that the survey that has been presented here is a very fragmentary and therefore in some ways a misleading one. Certain major figures—Kant, for example—have not been mentioned or have been inadequately discussed, and a certain distortion is introduced by the organization of this survey, as a projection backwards of certain ideas of contemporary interest rather than as a systematic presentation of the framework within which these ideas arose and found their place. Thus similarities have been stressed and divergences and conflicts overlooked. Still, even such a fragmentary survey as this does indicate, it seems to me, that the discontinuity of development in linguistic theory has been quite harmful to it and that a careful examination of classical linguistic theory, with its accompanying theory of mental processes, may prove to be an enterprise of considerable value.

Notes

1. M. Grammont, *Revue des langues Romanes*, vol. 60, p. 439. Quoted in G. Harnois, "Les théories du langage en France de 1660 à 1821," *Études Françaises*, vol. 17 (1929). Harnois in essence agrees, holding that earlier linguistics hardly merits the name "science" and that he is engaged in an "histoire de la linguistique, avant qu'il y ait une linguistique." Similar views have been widely voiced.

2. By a "generative grammar" I mean a description of the tacit competence of the speaker-hearer that underlies his actual performance in production and perception (understanding) of speech. A generative grammar, ideally, specifies a pairing of phonetic and semantic representations over an infinite range; it thus constitutes a hypothesis as to how the speaker-hearer interprets utterances, abstracting away from many factors that interweave with tacit competence to determine actual performance. For recent discussion, see Katz and Postal, *An Integrated Theory of Linguistic Descriptions* (Cambridge, M.I.T. Press, 1964); Chomsky, *Current Issues in Linguistic Theory* (The Hague, Mouton and Co., 1964); *Aspects of the Theory of Syntax* (Cambridge, M.I.T. Press, 1965).

3. Nor should it be assumed that the various contributors to what I will call "Cartesian linguistics" necessarily regarded themselves as constituting a single "tradition." This is surely not true. With the construct "Cartesian linguistics," I want to characterize a constellation of ideas and interests that appear in the tradition of "universal" or "philosophical grammar," which develops from the Port-Royal *Grammaire générale et raisonnée* (1660); in the general linguistics that developed during the romantic period and its immediate aftermath; and in the rationalist philosophy of mind that in part forms a common background for the two. That universal grammar has Cartesian origins is a commonplace; Sainte-Beuve, for example, refers to the Port-Royal theory of grammar as "une branche du Cartésianisme que Descartes n'avait pas lui-meme poussée (*Port-Royal*, vol. III, 1888, p. 539). An

association of the general linguistics of the romantic period to this complex is less immediately obvious, but I will try to show, nevertheless, that some of its central features (and, furthermore, those which seem to me to constitute its most valuable contribution) can be related to Cartesian antecedents.

By discussing romantic theories of language and mind within this framework, I am forced to exclude other important and characteristic aspects of these theories; for example, the organicism that was (rightly or wrongly) taken to be a reaction against Cartesian mechanism. In general, it must be emphasized that my concern here is not with the transmission of certain ideas and doctrines, but with their content and, ultimately, their contemporary significance.

A study of this sort could profitably be developed as part of a more general investigation of Cartesian linguistics as contrasted with a set of doctrines and assumptions that might be referred to as "empiricist linguistics" and illustrated by modern structural and taxonomic linguistics as well as by parallel developments in modern psychology and philosophy. I will not attempt to develop this distinction any more fully or clearly here, however.

4. It should be borne in mind that we are dealing with a period that antedates the divergence of linguistics, philosophy, and psychology. The insistence of each of these disciplines on "emancipating itself" from any contamination by the others is a peculiarly modern phenomenon. Again, current work in generative grammar returns to an earlier point of view, in this case, with respect to the place of linguistics among other studies.

5. He leaves open, as beyond the limitations of human reason, the question whether the explanatory hypotheses that he proposes are the "correct" ones in any absolute sense, limiting himself to the claim that they are adequate, though obviously not uniquely so. Cf. *Principles of Philosophy*, principle CCIV.

The context of this discussion of the limits of mechanical explanation must be kept clearly in mind. The issue is not the existence of mind, as a substance whose essence is thinking. To Descartes, this is obvious from introspection—more easily demonstrated, in fact, than the existence of body. What is at stake is the existence of other minds. This can be established only through indirect evidence of the sort that Descartes and his followers cite. These attempts to prove the existence of other minds were not too convincing to contemporary opinion. Pierre

Bayle, for example, characterizes the presumed inability of the Cartesians to prove the existence of other minds "as perhaps the weakest side of Cartesianism" ("Rorarius," in the *Historical and Critical Dictionary*, 1697, selections translated by Richard H. Popkin, Bobbs-Merrill, Indianapolis, 1965, p. 231).

6. *Discourse on Method*, part V. In *The Philosophical Works of Descartes*, translated by E. S. Haldane and G. R. T. Ross, vol. I, p. 116. The other quotations here are from pp. 116–117 of this edition.

In general, I will use English translations where these and the original are readily available and will cite the original otherwise, if available to me. In citing original sources, I will occasionally regularize spelling and punctuation slightly.

7. For some recent views and evidence on this question, see E. H. Lenneberg, "A Biological Perspective of Language," in *New Directions in the Study of Language*, edited by E. H. Lenneberg, M.I.T. Press, 1964.

8. Obviously, the properties of being unbounded and being stimulus-free are independent. An automaton may have only two responses that are produced randomly. A tape recorder or a person whose knowledge of a language extends only to the ability to take dictation has an unbounded output that is not stimulus-free in the intended sense. Animal behavior is typically regarded by the Cartesians as unbounded, but not stimulus-free, and hence not "creative" in the sense of human speech. Cf., for example, François Bayle, *The General System of the Cartesian Philosophy*, 1669 (English translation dated 1670, p. 63): "And because there may be an infinite variety in the impressions made by the objects upon the senses, there may also be an innumerable variety in the determination of the Spirits to flow into the Muscles, and by consequence, an infinite variety in the Motions of Animals; and that the more, because there is a greater variety of parts, and more contrivance and art in the structure." The unboundedness of human speech, as an expression of limitless thought, is an entirely different matter, because of the freedom from stimulus control and the appropriateness to new situations.

It is important to distinguish "appropriateness of behavior to situations" from "control of behavior by stimuli." The latter is characteristic of automata; it is the former that is held to be beyond the bounds of mechanical explanation, in its full human variety.

Modern studies of animal communication so far offer no counterevidence to the Cartesian assumption that human language is based on an entirely distinct principle. Each known animal communication system either consists of a fixed number of signals, each associated with a specific range of eliciting conditions or internal states, or a fixed number of "linguistic dimensions," each associated with a nonlinguistic dimension in the sense that selection of a point along one indicates a corresponding point along the other. In neither case is there any significant similarity to human language. Human and animal communication fall together only at a level of generality that includes almost all other behavior as well.

9. In general, then, "although machines can perform certain things as well as or perhaps better than any of us can do, they infallibly fall short in others, by the which means we may discover that they did not act from knowledge, but only from the disposition of their organs." There are, then, two "very certain tests" by which we can determine whether a device is really human, the one provided by the creative aspect of language use, the other, by the diversity of human action. "It is virtually impossible (in the Haldane-Ross translation, "morally impossible") that there should be sufficient diversity in any machine to allow it to act in all the events of life in the same way as our reason causes us to act." In taking this position, Descartes expands on his conception of the "cognitive power" as a faculty which is not purely passive and which "is properly called mind when it either forms new ideas in the fancy or attends to those already formed," acting in a way that is not completely under the control of sense or imagination or memory (*Rules for the Direction of the Mind*, 1628; Haldane and Ross, p. 39). Still earlier, Descartes remarks that "from the very perfection of animal actions we suspect that they do not have free will" (c. 1620; cited by L. C. Rosenfield, *From Beast-Machine to Man-Machine*, New York, Oxford Univ. Press, 1941, p. 3, as the first reference by Descartes to the problem of animal soul).

The idea that the "cognitive power" is properly called "mind" only when it is in some sense creative has earlier origins. One source that might well have been familiar to Descartes is Juan Huarte's *Examen de Ingenios* (1575), which was widely translated and circulated (I quote from the English translation by Bellamy, 1698). Huarte understands the word *Ingenio* to have the root meaning "engender," "generate"—he relates it to *gigno, genero, ingenero* (p. 2). Thus "one may discover two generative Powers in Man, one common with the Beasts and Plants, and the other Participating of Spiritual Substances, God and the Angels" (p. 3). "Wit [Ingenio] is a generative power . . . the Understanding is a Generative Faculty" (p. 3). As distinct from divine "Genius," the human "rational soul" and "spiritual substances" do not have "sufficient Force and Power in their Generation to give real being to what they Ingender" but only "to produce an accident in the Memory," "an Idea and Image of what we know and understand" that must be given concrete existence by work and art (pp. 4–5). Similarly the arts and sciences are "a sort of Images, and Figures, begotten by [men's] Minds in their Memory, which represent to the Life the Posture and natural Composition of the Subject relating to the intended Science" (p. 6). One who learns some subject must "Engender within himself an entire and true Figure" that represents its principles and structure (p. 6). Truly active minds will be "such, that assisted by the subject only, [they will] without the help of any Body, produce a thousand Conceits they never heard spoke of" (p. 7). The empiricist maxim, "That there is nothing in the Understanding, but what has past through the Sense," attributed to Aristotle, applies only to "docile wits" that lack this capacity. Although the "perfect wit" is only an ideal case, "yet it must be granted, we have observ'd many Persons approach very near it, inventing and saying such things as they never heard from their Masters, nor any Mouth" (p. 16). There is even a third kind of wit "by means of which, some have without Art or Study spoke such subtle and surprizing things, and yet true, that were never before seen, heard, or writ, no nor ever so much as thought of" and which may involve "a mixture of Madness" (p. 17); these three types of wit involve the memory, understanding, and imagination, respectively. In general, "all [man's] Honour and Nobility, as *Cicero* observed, consists in his being favour'd with, and having an Eloquent Tongue: *As Wit is the Ornament of a Man, so Eloquence is the Light and Beauty of Wit.* In this alone he distinguishes himself from the Brutes, and approaches near to God, as being the greatest Glory which is possible to be obtained in Nature" (p. 22). The most severe "disability of wit," under which men "differ not at all from Brute Beasts," is the disability, which "very much resembles that of Eunuchs . . . unable for Generation," that prevents the rational faculty from arriving at "the first Principles of all Arts implanted in the Scholar's Mind, before he begin to learn, for which the Wit can give no other proofs of itself, than to receive them as things already known; and if he be not able to form an Idea of them in his Mind, we may strongly conclude him wholly incapable of the Sciences." In this case, "neither the Lash of the Rod, nor his Cries, nor Method, nor Examples, nor Time, nor Experience, nor any thing in Nature can sufficiently Excite him to bring forth any thing" (p. 27–28).

See K. Gunderson, "Descartes, La Mettrie, Language and Machines," *Philosophy*, vol. 39, pp. 193–222 (1964), for an interesting discussion of Descartes's arguments as related to contemporary discussions of "intelligence" of automata. For general background on the development and critique of Descartes's theory of the extent and limits of mechanical explanation, see Rosenfield, *op. cit.*, and H. Kirkinen, "Les origines de la conception moderne de l'homme-machine," *Annales Academiae Scientiarum Fennicae*, ser. B, vol. 122, Helsinki (1961).

10. Translated (in part) in H. A. P. Torrey, *The Philosophy of Descartes*, New York, Holt (1892), pp. 281–284.

11. That is, by conditioning. When animals are taught "by art," their actions are produced with reference to a passion, in the sense that this behavior is associated with the "stir of expectation of something to eat" or the "motions of their fear, their hope, or their joy" that constitute the original contingency for the teaching. Descartes is therefore pointing out that, just as in its normal use "verbal behavior" is free of identifiable external stimuli or internal physiological states, so it is evidently not developed in the individual by conditioning. He does not elaborate on this, regarding it perhaps as too obvious to merit discussion. It is noteworthy that modern behaviorist speculation about human learning denies these truisms. For some discussion, see Chomsky, "Review of Skinner, 'Verbal Behavior,'" *Language*, vol. 35, pp. 26–58; *Aspects of the Theory of Syntax*, chap. 1, §8; J. Katz, *Philosophy of Language*, Harper & Row, 1966; J. Fodor, "Could Meaning be an 'r_m,'" *Journal of Verbal Learning and Verbal Behavior*, vol. 4, pp. 73–81 (1965).

12. Torrey, *The Philosophy of Descartes*, pp. 284–287. The Descartes-More correspondence, in so far as it relates to animal automatism, is translated in full by L. C. Rosenfield (L. Cohen). in the *Annals of Science*, vol. 1, no. 1 (1936).

13. Descartes goes on to explain that he does not deny to animals life or sensation or even feeling, in so far as it depends only on the bodily organs.

14. *Discours Physique de la Parole*, 1666. Page references are to the second edition, 1677. There is an English translation, dated 1668. Rosenfield remarks that Cordemoy develops Descartes's argument involving lack of true speech among animals so fully that after him "the point was given very little attention, as if subsequent authors considered this the last word on the subject" (*From Beast-Machine to Man-Machine*, p. 40).

15. There is no problem, for Cordemoy (as for Descartes), in determining whether he himself possesses a soul, since it is evident to him, by introspection, "que certaines pensées accompagnoient toujours en moy la pluspart des mouvemens de mes organes" (p. 3).

16. La Mettrie, *L'Homme Machine*, 1747. A critical edition with notes and background material was published by A. Vartanian, Princeton University Press (1960). The translations given here are from *Man a Machine*, La Salle, Ill., Open Court (1912); page references are to the 1961 edition, which contains a French text with English translation.

17. Père G. H. Bougeant, *Amusement philosophique sur le langage des bestes* (1739).

18. This is not to deny that the method of explanation suggested by La Mettrie may be in principle correct. What concerns me here is not the adequacy of the proposed explanations of Descartes and others, but the observations on human language that elicited these attempts.

19. G. Ryle, *The Concept of Mind*, Hutchinson's University Library, London (1949). See J. Fodor, "Is Psychology Possible?" chap. 1 of *Psychological Explanation* (Random House, forthcoming), for a critique of the views of Ryle and others regarding psychological explanation.

20. These are described in terms of "powers," "propensities," and "dispositions," which are characterized only through scattered examples. These constitute a new "myth" as mysterious and poorly understood as Descartes's "mental substance."

21. L. Bloomfield, *Language*, New York, Holt (1933), p. 275. When a speaker produces speech forms that he has not heard, "we say that he utters them *on the analogy* of similar forms which he has heard." For Bloomfield, human language differs from animal communication systems in no fundamental way, but only by its

"great differentiation." Otherwise, its function is similar. "Man utters many kinds of vocal noise and makes use of the variety: under certain types of stimuli he produces certain vocal sounds, and his fellows, hearing these same sounds, make the appropriate response" (p. 27). He holds that "language is a matter of training and habit" (p. 34) and that with careful statistical investigation "we should doubtless be able to foretell how many times any given utterance . . . would be spoken within a fixed number of days" (p. 37) (a conclusion that is certainly correct, since for almost all normal utterances the predicted number would be zero).

22. C. F. Hockett, *A Course in Modern Linguistics*, New York, Macmillan (1958), §§36, 50. He remarks that "it has been said that whenever a person speaks, he is either mimicking or analogizing," and he accepts this view, stating that "when we hear a fairly long and involved utterance which is evidently not a direct quotation, we can be reasonably certain that analogy is at work" (p. 425). Among modern linguists, Hockett is unusual in that he has at least noticed that a problem exists.

In discussing innovation, Hockett seems to imply that novel expressions can be understood only through reference to context (p. 303). In fact, failure to consider the linguistic mechanisms that determine the meaning of the ordinary, generally quite novel sentences of everyday life is typical of modern linguistics.

23. Modern discussions of the difference between human language and animal communication systems occasionally recapture some of the Cartesian insights. See, for example, L. Carmichael, "The Early Growth of Language Capacity in the Individual," in Lenneberg (ed.), *op. cit.*

24. J. G. Herder, *Abhandlung über den Ursprung der Sprache* (1772). This is now available, in part, in E. Heintel (ed.), *Herder's Sprachphilosophie*, Hamburg, Felix Meiner Verlag (1960), pp. 1–87. Page references are to this volume.

25. This is true as well of the development of language in the individual. Study of the "origin of language" is essentially a study of the "essence of language," in this period, and the growth of language in the individual and its growth in the nation are often taken to be parallel in their general characteristics. Cf. A. W. Schlegel, *Die Kunstlehre* (1801; Stuttgart, W. Kohlhammer Verlag, 1963, p. 234): in the discovery of language by children, "es

wiederholt sich bei ihnen in schwachen Spuren immer noch das, was bei der Erfindung der Sprache durch das Menschengeschlecht überhaupt vorging"; in general, "es gehört . . . zur Erlernung einer Sprache dieselbe Fähigkeit, die bei ihrer Erfindung nur in höherem Grade wirksam ist" (p. 235). Under the influence of Humboldt, H. Steinthal goes even further and states that "Der Unterschied zwischen der Urschöpfung und der täglich wiederholten existirt . . . rücksichtlich der Sprache gar nicht" (*Grammatik, Logik und Psychologie*, Berlin, 1855, p. 232).

26. *Discourse on Method*, p. 116 of Haldane and Ross.

27. Descartes does not restrict language to purely intellectual function in a narrow sense. See, for example, *Principles of Philosophy*, principle CXCVII (Haldane and Ross, p. 294):

> We observe that words, whether uttered by the voice or merely written, excite in our minds all sorts of thoughts and emotions . . . we can trace letters which bring to the minds of our readers thoughts of battles, tempests or furies, and the emotions of indignation and sadness; while if the pen be moved in another way, . . . thoughts may be given of quite a different kind, viz. those of quietude, peace, pleasantness, and the quite opposite passions of love and joy.

28. *Treatise the Third: Concerning Happiness, a Dialogue* (1741). In Harris's *Works*, edited by the Earl of Malmesbury, London (1801), vol. I, p. 94.

29. In this discussion, Harris appears to be making the gratuitous assumption, typical of the modern variants of this doctrine, that, since man is capable of "infinite directions," he is therefore completely plastic; that is, the assumption that innate factors govern his intellectual development only marginally, if at all. Obviously this further assumption has no connection to the observation regarding freedom from the control of instinct and drives and regarding the infinite range of potential skill and knowledge. With this independent assumption, Harris is, of course, very much outside of the framework of Cartesian thought.

Elsewhere, Harris expresses himself in a manner which is susceptible to a rather different interpretation. In discussing the interplay between creative genius and rule (*Philological Inquiries*, 1780, in *Works*, vol. II), he rejects the view "that *Geniuses*, tho' *prior to Systems*, were *prior also to Rules* [e.g., the unities of time and place, in the theory of drama], because *RULES* from the beginning *existed in their own Minds,* and were a part of that *immutable Truth,* which is eternal and everywhere" (p. 409). Genius and rules are "so *reciprocally* connected, that 'tis *GENIUS* which discovers *Rules* [these being implicit in the mind]; and then *RULES,* which govern *Genius.*"

30. One would not refer to an act as "creative" simply on the basis of its novelty and independence of identifiable drives or stimuli. Hence the term "creative aspect of language use" is not entirely appropriate, without qualification, as a designation for the property of ordinary language that concerned Descartes and Cordemoy.

It is interesting, in this connection, to note that Galileo described the discovery of a means to communicate one's "most secret thoughts to any other person . . . with no greater difficulty than the various collocations of twenty-four little characters upon a paper" as the greatest of all human inventions, comparable with the creations of a Michelangelo, a Raphael, or a Titian (*Dialogue on the Great World Systems,* 1630, University of Chicago Press, 1953, pp. 116–117). I am indebted for this reference to E. H. Gombrich.

Compare the reference in the *Grammaire générale et raisonnée* to "cette invention merveilleuse de composer de 25 ou 30 sons cette infinie de mots, qui n'ayant rien de semblable en eux-mesmes, à ce qui se passe dans notre esprit, ne laissent pas d'en découvrir aux autres tout le secret, et de faire entendre à ceux qui n'y peuvent penetrer, tout ce que nous concevons, et tous les divers mouvemens de notre ame" (p. 27).

31. Cf. note 25. References are to pp. 233–234 of the edition cited there, which is vol. II of a collection of *Kritische Schriften und Briefe.*

32. *Briefe über Poesie, Silbenmass und Sprache* (1795). In *Sprache und Poetik,* vol. I of *Kritische Schriften und Briefe,* Stuttgart, W. Kohlhammer Verlag (1962), p. 152.

33. " . . . die natürlichen Medien der Kunst sind Handlungen, wodurch der Mensch sein Inneres äusserlich offenbart" (*Die Kunstlehre,* p. 230—the only such means are "Worte, Töne, und Gebärden"); therefore it is natural for Schlegel to conclude that language itself is a primordial art form and that it is, further, "von ihrer Entstehung an der Urstoff der Poesie" (p. 232).

34. For Schlegel (*Die Kunstlehre,* p. 225), "Die Kunst" is "ein schrankenloser Gedanke" and is thus indefinable; "ihr Zweck,

d.h. die Richtung ihres Strebens kann wohl im allgemeinen an-
gedeutet werden; aber was sie im Laufe der Zeiten realisiren soll
und kann, vermag kein Verstandesbegriff zu umfassen, denn es
ist unendlich." The passage that is paraphrased in the text then
continues as follows:

> Bei der Poesie findet es aber in noch höherem Grade statt;
> denn die übrigen Künste haben doch nach ihren beschränkten
> Medien oder Mitteln der Darstellung eine bestimmte Sphäre,
> die sich einigermassen ausmessen lässt. Das Medium der Poesie
> aber ist eben dasselbe, wodurch der menschliche Geist
> überhaupt zur Besinnung gelangt, und seine Vorstellungen
> zu willkürlicher Verknüpfung und Äusserung in die Gewalt
> bekommt: die Sprache. Daher ist sie auch nicht an Gegen-
> stände gebunden, sondern sie schafft sich die ihrigen selbst;
> sie ist die umfassendste aller Künste, und gleichsam der in
> ihnen überall gegenwärtige Universalgeist. Dasjenige in den
> Darstellungen der übrigen Künste, was uns über die gewöhn-
> liche Wirklichkeit in eine Welt der Phantasie erhebt, nennt
> man das Poetische in ihnen; Poesie bezeichnet also in diesem
> Sinne überhaupt die künstlerische Erfindung, den wunderbaren
> Akt, wodurch dieselbe die Natur bereichert; wie der Name
> aussagt, eine wahre Schöpfung und Hervorbringung. Jeder
> äusseren materiellen Darstellung geht eine innere in dem Geiste
> des Künstlers voran, bei welcher die Sprache immer als
> Vermittlerin des Bewusstseins eintritt, und folglich kann man
> sagen, dass jene jederzeit aus dem Schosse der Poesie her-
> vorgeht. Die Sprache ist kein Produkt der Natur, sondern
> ein Abdruck des menschlichen Geistes, der darin die Ent-
> stehung und Verwandtschaft seiner Vorstellungen und den
> ganzen Mechanismus seiner Operationen niederlegt. Es wird
> also in der Poesie schon Gebildetes wieder gebildet; und die
> Bildsamkeit ihres Organs ist ebenso grenzenlos als die Fähigkeit
> des Geistes zur Rückkehr auf sich selbst durch immer höhere
> potenziertere Reflexionen.

35. For further discussion of the character, sources, and general development of romantic aesthetic theory, see M. H. Abrams, *The
Mirror and the Lamp*, Oxford University Press (1953). There is
some discussion of the philosophy of language of romanticism
in the first volume of E. Cassirer, *The Philosophy of Symbolic
Forms* (1923; English translation, Yale University Press, 1953).

See also E. Fiesel, *Die Sprachphilosophie der deutschen Romantik,* Tübingen, Verlag von J. C. B. Mohr (1927).

36. In particular, in his *Über die Verschiedenheit des Menschlichen Sprachbaues,* published posthumously in 1836. A facsimile edition appeared in 1960 (F. Dümmlers Verlag, Bonn). Page references here are to this edition. Parts are translated into English in M. Cowan, *Humanist without Portfolio,* Detroit, Wayne State University Press (1963). A full translation and commentary are in preparation by J. Viertel. Backgrounds of Humboldt's linguistic theories are discussed in R. L. Brown, *Some Sources and Aspects of Wilhelm von Humboldt's Conception of Linguistic Relativity,* unpublished University of Illinois doctoral dissertation (1964).

Bloomfield refers to Humboldt's treatise as "the first great book on general linguistics" (*Language,* p. 18). Considered against the background that we are surveying here, it seems to mark the terminal point of the development of Cartesian linguistics rather than the beginning of a new era of linguistic thought. See Chomsky, *Current Issues in Linguistic Theory,* for some discussion of Humboldtian general linguistics, its relation to the work of the following century, and its reemergence in contemporary studies of language and cognition.

37. The German translations are Humboldt's. These concepts of Humboldt's do not seem to me to be entirely clear, and I will focus attention here on one aspect of them. That a single consistent interpretation of these notions is clearly determined by the text is not obvious. Despite this qualification, it seems safe to conclude that what will be outlined here is at least one of the central strands in Humboldt's thought. I am indebted to J. Viertel for many observations and suggestions regarding the interpretation of the text.

38. For Humboldt, to speak of a word in a language as "articulated" is to refer it to the system of underlying elements from which it is constructed, elements that could be used to form infinitely many other words according to definite intuitions and rules. It is in this sense that a word is an "articulated object," grasped, in perception, by the exercise of the "menschliche Sprachkraft" rather than by some process analogous simply to "das thierische Empfindungsvermögen." See p. 71:

> Nun ist aber dasjenige, was die *Articulation* dem blossen Hervorrufen seiner Bedeutung . . . [i.e., of the meaning of a

perceived word] . . . hinzufügt, dass sie das Wort unmittelbar durch seine Form als einen Theil eines unendlichen Ganzen, einer Sprache, darstellt. Denn es ist durch sie, auch in einzelnen Wörtern, die Möglichkeit gegeben, aus den Elementen dieser eine wirklich bis ins Unbestimmte gehende Anzahl anderer Wörter nach bestimmenden Gefühlen und Regeln zu bilden, und dadurch unter allen Wörtern eine Verwandtschaft, entsprechend der Verwandtschaft der Begriffe, zu stiften.

He then clarifies his meaning further, pointing out that it is only the generative processes that are grasped by the mind, and that language cannot be regarded

als ein daliegender, in seinem Ganzen übersehbarer, oder nach und nach mitheilbarer Stoff, sondern muss als ein sich ewig *erzeugender* angesehen werden, wo die Gesetze der Erzeugung bestimmt sind, aber der Umfang und gewissermassen auch die Art des Erzeugnisses gänzlich unbestimmt bleiben.

Compare A. W. Schlegel's definition of "articulation" (*Kunstlehre*, p. 239):

Das Artikulieren (Gliedern der Rede gleichsam) besteht in willkürlichen absichtlichen Bewegungen der Organe und entspricht also ähnlichen Handlungen des Geistes.

He points out that articulated language is different in kind from animal cries or expressions of emotion—that it cannot be approached by a series of "crude imitations" but requires a new principle.

See also note 30.

39. See p. 58: "Das in dieser Arbeit des Geistes, den articulirten Laut zum Gedankenausdruck zu erheben, liegende Beständige und Gleichförmige, so vollständig, als möglich, in seinem Zusammenhange aufgefasst, und systematisch dargestellt, macht die *Form der Sprache* aus." It seems to me that Humboldt's "form of language" is essentially what would in current terminology be called "the generative grammar" of a language, in the broadest sense in which this term has been used. See note 2 and pp. 38–39, below.

40. For example, the lingua franca of the Mediterranean coast; or, we may add, animal communication systems or "language games" of the sort referred to by Bougeant, Bloomfield, Wittgenstein,

and many others and proposed by them as typical and paradigmatic—as the "primitive forms" of language.

41. In identifying a particular state of a language as an object of description with "psychological reality," we depart from Humboldt, who is extremely unclear about the relation of synchronic to diachronic description.

42. In his *Hermes*, Harris perhaps comes closest to the Humboldtian conception of "form" in a citation from Ammonius, which relates motion to dance, timber to a door, and "the power of producing a vocal sound" (as the material basis for speech) to "that of explaining ourselves by Nouns, or Verbs" (as its form, which derives from man's unique soul as the material basis derives from nature). Cf. Harris, *Works*, vol. I, p. 393, footnote.

Elsewhere, in another connection, Harris discusses a conception of "form" that is much richer, however. In his *Philosophical Arrangements* (1775; *Works*, vol. II) he develops the notion of "form" as "animating principle": "the animating form of a natural body is neither its organization, nor its figure, nor any other of these inferior forms, which make up the system of its visible qualities; but 'tis the power, which, not being that organization, nor that figure, nor those qualities, is yet able to produce, to preserve, and to employ them" (p. 59).

43. *Lectures on Dramatic Art and Literature* (1808), translated by John Black, p. 340 of the second edition, London, George Bell and Sons (1892).

44. "Lectures and Notes of 1818," in T. Ashe (ed.), *Lectures and Notes on Shakespeare and other English Poets*, George Bell and Sons (1893), p. 229. Some of Coleridge's comments on the nature of mind foreshadow Humboldt's observations on language in their emphasis on the diversity of creative potential within the bounds of finite rules. In the same lecture he denies that genius must be opposed to rule (again paraphrasing Schlegel—cf. also note 29) and argues that "no work of true genius dares want its appropriate [organic] form." "As it must not, so genius cannot be lawless: for it is even this that constitutes its genius—the power of acting creatively under laws of its own origination."

Elsewhere, he states that "the mind does not resemble an Aeolian harp, nor even a barrel organ turned by a stream of water, conceive as many tunes mechanized in it as you like, but rather as far as objects are concerned a violin or other instrument of few strings yet vast compass, played on by a musician of Genius" (quoted by R. Wellek, *Kant in England*, Princeton University Press, 1931, p. 82). For much additional relevant material, see Abrams, *op. cit.*

45. It should be noted that this topic does not seem to have been raised in any explicit way in the Schlegel-Humboldt correspondence. See A. Leitzmann (ed.), *Briefwechsel zwischen W. von Humboldt und A. W. Schlegel* (1908). This correspondence contains much discussion of "organic" and "mechanical" form but in a different connection, namely, with reference to the relation between inflection and agglutination as linguistic processes, a topic that is also developed at length in Humboldt's *Über die Verschiedenheit des menschlichen Sprachbaues.*

The question of how the form of language arises from and determines individual "creative" acts is a not uncommon one during this period. Cf., for example, Coleridge: "What a magnificent History of acts of individual minds, sanctioned by the collective Mind of the Country a Language is . . . a chaos grinding itself into compatibility." Quoted in A. D. Snyder, *Coleridge on Logic and Learning*, Yale University Press (1929), p. 138.

46. The significance and origins of this notion are described in R. Berthelot, *Science et philosophie chez Goethe*, Paris, F. Alcan (1932), and R. Magnus, *Goethe als Naturforscher*, Leipzig, Barth (1906), translated by H. Norden, Henry Schuman, Inc., New York (1949). As is well known, the concept of organic form develops in biology, as well as in philosophy and criticism, during the period that we are now reviewing. Compare, for example, Schlegel's notion of organic form with Blumenbach's concept of "Bildungstrieb" in biology, namely, the concept of a living, generative, formative principle internal to an organism that determines its ontogenesis and leads it from germ to adult (cf. Berthelot, p. 42; he states that this influenced Kant's similar formulations in the *Critique of Judgment*). Berthelot characterizes Schelling's Naturphilosophie as conceiving of nature "comme une transformation dynamique qualitative produisant des formes nouvelles, irreductibles aux formes antérieures, par l'action d'une activité spontanée, interne et primitivement inconsciente" (p. 40). Many other references might be given to illustrate the parallel and interplay. These matters are discussed in various places, e.g., A. O. Lovejoy, *The Great Chain of Being*, New York, Harper & Row (1936); Abrams, *op. cit.* For further background and many references, see E. Mendelsohn, "The

Biological Sciences in the Nineteenth Century: Some Problems and Sources," *History of Science*, vol. 3, pp. 39–59 (1964).

47. Quoted in Magnus, *op. cit.*, p. 59. Lovejoy, *op. cit.*, traces the idea of a logical "Urbild" to J. B. Robinet's *De la Nature* (1761–1768). He quotes Robinet (p. 279) as defining the notion "prototype" as "un principe intellectuel qui ne s'altère qu'en se réalisant dans la matière"; this notion Robinet then elaborated with respect to all animate and even inanimate nature.

48. The title of Humboldt's major work should not lead one to assume that he would be sympathetic to the view that each language is a unique historical product that may, in principle, have any imaginable structure. This view, in one form or another, has been expressed by many post-Humboldtian linguists. To mention just the temporal extremes, it can be illustrated by W. D. Whitney's critique of Humboldtian linguistics ("Steinthal and the Psychological Theory of Language," *North American Review*, 1872; reprinted in *Oriental and Linguistic Studies*, New York, Scribner, Armstrong and Co., 1874), in which he concludes that "the infinite diversity of human speech ought alone to be a sufficient bar to the assertion that an understanding of the powers of the soul involves the explanation of speech" (p. 360 in *Oriental and Linguistic Studies*) and that language is strictly a "historical product," nothing other than "the sum of words and phrases by which any man expresses his thought" (p. 372); or M. Joos' summary of what he calls the "Boasian" tradition of American linguistics as adopting the view "that languages could differ from each other without limit and in unpredictable ways" (M. Joos, ed., *Readings in Linguistics*, American Council of Learned Societies, Washington, 1957, p. 96). Humboldt, in contrast, repeatedly expresses his opinion that, in their general structural features, languages are cast to the same mold. It seems to me that he is consistent in adopting the position that he expresses clearly in a letter to A. W. Schlegel (1822, cf. Leitzmann, *op. cit.*, p. 54): "Dass alle Sprachen in Absicht der Grammatik sich sehr ähnlich sehen, wenn man sie nicht oberflächlich, sondern tief in ihrem Innern untersucht, ist unläugbar." Furthermore, this is clearly the only view compatible with his Platonistic theory of language acquisition (cf. p. 64, below).

See Chomsky, *Current Issues in Linguistic Theory*, for some further discussion of the historical importance of Whitney's influential but (in my opinion) utterly wrong-headed and superficial critique.

49. As emphasized by H. Steinthal in his *Gedächtnissrede auf Humboldt an seinem hundertjahrigen Geburtstage* (Berlin, 1867).

50. R. Rocker, *Nationalism and Culture*, translated by R. E. Chase, London, Freedom Press (1937). This judgment is based largely on Humboldt's early essay *Ideen zu einem Versuch die Grenzen der Wirksamkeit des Staats zu bestimmen* (1792). Parts of this are translated in Cowan, *op. cit.*, pp. 37–64.

51. The political meaning of a "natural rights" doctrine such as Humboldt's depends very much on the exact way in which it is phrased and the social context in which it appears, and an evaluation of these questions, in the present case, raises many problems. The terms in which Humboldt frames this doctrine suggest a comparison with Marx's *Economic and Philosophic Manuscripts* (1844; translated by T. B. Bottomore, in E. Fromm, ed., *Marx's Concept of Man*, New York, Ungar, 1961), with their description of the "alienation of labor when work is *external* to the worker, . . . not part of his nature . . . [so that] . . . he does not fulfill himself in his work but denies himself . . . [and is] . . . physically exhausted and mentally debased" (p. 98) and their definition of the "species-character" of human beings as "free, conscious activity" and "productive life" (p. 101), of which man is deprived by the alienated labor that "casts some of the workers back into a barbarous kind of work and turns others into machines" (p. 97), as well as with Marx's well-known reference to a higher form of society in which "labor has become not only a means of life, but also the highest want in life" (*Critique of the Gotha Program*, 1875).

Humboldt's remarks might be compared with Rousseau's critique of modern social institutions in the *Discourse on the Origins and Foundations of Inequality among Men* (1755; translated in R. D. Masters, ed., *The First and Second Discourses*, New York, St Martin's, 1964). Rousseau's goal is "to set forth the origin and progress of inequality, the establishment and abuse of political societies, insofar as these things can be deduced from the nature of man by the light of reason alone, and independently of the sacred dogmas which give to sovereign authority the sanction of divine right" (p. 180). Along strictly Cartesian lines, he characterizes an animal as "only an ingenious machine to which nature has given senses in order to revitalize itself and guarantee itself, to a certain point, from all that tends to destroy or upset it." "Every animal has ideas, since it has senses; it even combines its ideas up to a certain point, and in this regard man differs from a beast only in degree" (cf. note 13). What distinguishes man from beast in an absolute way is that man is a "free agent" and has "the consciousness of this freedom" (a further specific difference, perhaps reducible to man's freedom, is his "faculty of self-perfection," as an individual and a species). Although much in man's nature can be attributed to properties of "the human machine," still man's behavior is uniquely beyond the bounds of physical explanation. "For physics explains in some way the mechanism of the senses and the formation of ideas; but in the power of willing, or rather of choosing, and in the sentiment of this power are found only spiritual acts about which the laws of mechanics explain nothing" (p. 113f.).

From this essentially Cartesian picture of human nature, Rousseau develops his theory and evaluation of modern society. Since freedom is "the most noble of man's faculties," one is "degrading one's nature, putting oneself on the level of beasts enslaved by instinct" by renouncing freedom and subjecting oneself to the dictates of a "ferocious or insane master" (p. 167). The national state, modern social organization, and conventional law all originate in a kind of conspiracy by the rich and powerful to preserve and institutionalize power and property, a conspiracy that "gave new fetters to the weak and new forces to the rich, destroyed natural freedom for all time, established forever the law of property and inequality, changed a clever usurpation into an irrevocable right, and for the profit of a few ambitious men henceforth subjected the whole human race to work, servitude, and misery." Finally, with the establishment of the national state, "the most decent men learned to consider it one of their duties to murder their fellow-men; at length men were seen to massacre each other by the thousands without knowing why" (pp. 160–161). In so far as society institutionalizes property rights, magistracy, and arbitrary power, it violates natural law (pp. 168ff.). It is contrary to natural right and against the law of nature that "a handful of men be glutted with superfluities while the starving multitude lacks necessities" (p. 181) or that "each man finds his profit in the misfortune of others" (p. 194); "and the jurists, who have gravely pronounced that the child of a slave would be born a slave, have decided in other terms that a man would not be born a man" (p. 168). Man has become mere "sociable man," living "outside of himself" and "only in the opinion of others," from whose judgment alone "he draws the sentiment of his existence" (p. 179). He can regain true humanity only by abolishing the status of rich and poor, powerful and weak, master and slave—by "new revolutions" that will "dissolve the government altogether or bring it closer to its legitimate institution" (p. 172); "the uprising that ends by strangling or dethroning a sultan is as lawful an act as those by which he disposed, the day before, of the lives and goods of his subjects" (p. 177).

52. N. S. Troubetzkoy, "La phonologie actuelle," *Psychologie de langage*, Paris (1933), p. 245.

53. This notion seems to have developed in connection with the controversy over use of the vernacular to replace Latin. Cf. F. Brunot, *Histoire de la langue Française*, Paris, Librarie Armand Colin, IV (1924), pp. 1104f., and G. Sahlin, *César Chesneau du Marsais et son rôle dans l'évolution de la Grammaire générale*, Paris, Presses-Universitaires (1928), pp. 88–89, for some early references, including one to a 1669 source that goes so far, in defense of the naturalness of French, as to claim that "les Romains pensoient en François devant que de parler en Latin." Diderot is so convinced of the "naturalness" of French that he regards it as more suitable for science than for literature, the other European languages, "unnatural" in their word order, being more suited for literary expression (*Lettre sur les sourds et muets*, 1751). Englishmen tended to have a different view of the matter. Bentham, for example, held that "of all known languages, English is . . . that in which, in the highest degree, taken in the aggregate, the most important of the properties desirable in every language are to be found" (*Works*, edited by J. Bowring, New York, Russell and Russell, Inc., 1962, vol. VIII, p. 342). Huarte, writing in the late sixteenth century, took for granted "the Analogy and Correspondence between the Latin Tongue, and the Rational Soul": "*Latin* words, and the manner of speaking this Tongue, are so Rational, and so agreeably strike the Ear, that the Rational Soul meeting with the Temperament necessary to invent a very eloquent Language, immediately stumbles on the Latin" (*op. cit.*, p. 122).

From the seventeenth century, there was much discussion of the possibility of inventing a "philosophical language" that would reflect "la vraie philosophie" and the principles of thought better than any actual human language. An interest in this problem is apparently at the roots of Leibniz's interest in comparative grammar, which might reveal the "excellencies of language." For discussion of these developments, see Couturat and Leau, *Histoire de la langue universelle*, (Paris, 1903); Margaret M. C. McIntosh, *The Phonetic and Linguistic Theory of the Royal Society School*, from Wallis to Cooper, unpublished bachelor of letters thesis, Oxford University (1956); Cassirer, *The Philosophy of Symbolic Forms*.

54. B. Lamy, *De l'Art de Parler* (1676). There are, however, stylistic reasons that may lead one to invert the "ordre naturel" in many languages; not, however, in French, which does not, he maintains, make use of such "figures de Grammaire," since "elle aime la netteté et la naïveté; c'est pourquoi elle exprime les choses autant qu'il se peut dans l'ordre le plus naturel, et le plus simple" (p. 23). Cf. also pp. 26–27.

55. J. Wilkins, *An Essay towards a Real Character and a Philosophical Language* (1668).

56. The assumption of a "natural order," however, has the advantage that it does not fly in the face of the facts quite so obviously as the belief that language can be described in terms of "habits" or "dispositions to respond" or that the syntactic structure of a language is some sort of list of patterns. It is, therefore, not excluded that the notion of "natural order" can be clarified and developed as a hypothesis of some significance regarding language structure.

57. Leibniz, *Nouveaux essais sur l'entendment humain*, book III, chap. VII; translated into English by A. G. Langley, La Salle, Illinois, Open Court Publishing Co. He goes on to maintain that "an exact analysis of the signification of words would show us better than anything else the workings of the understanding" (p. 368 of the 1949 edition). For further discussion of Leibniz's concern with language, see H. Aarslef, "Leibniz on Locke on Language," *American Philosophical Quarterly*, vol. 1, no. 3, pp. 1–24 (1964).

58. F. Schlegel, *Geschichte der alten und neuen Literatur* (1812); cited by Fiesel, *op. cit.*, p. 8. See also A. W. Schlegel, "De l'étymologie en général," in E. Böcking (ed.), *Oeuvres écrites en Français*, Leipzig (1846), p. 133: "On a dit souvent que la grammaire est la logique mise en pratique; il y a plus: c'est une analyse profonde, une métaphysique subtile de la pensée."

59. Occasionally, from quite unexpected sources. For example, Proudhon's scholarship application to the Besançon Academy, in 1837,

announced his intention of developing a general grammar in which he hoped to "chercher à la psychologie de nouvelles régions, à la philosophie de nouvelles voies; étudier la nature et le mécanisme de l'esprit humain dans la plus apparente et la plus saisissable de ses facultés, la parole; déterminer, d'après l'origine et les procédés du langage, la source et la filiation des croyances humaines; appliquer, en un mot, la grammaire à la métaphysique et à la morale, et réaliser une pensée qui tourmente de profonds génies . . ." (*Correspondance de P.-J. Proudhon*, vol. I, edited by J.-A. Langlois, Paris, Librarie Internationale, 1875, p. 31). Cf. also J. S. Mill: "Grammar . . . is the beginning of the analysis of the thinking process. The principles and rules of grammar are the means by which the forms of language are made to correspond with the universal forms of thought. The distinctions between the various parts of speech, between the cases of nouns, the moods and tenses of verbs, the functions of particles, are distinctions in thought, not merely in words. . . . The structure of every sentence is a lesson in logic" (Rectorial Address at St. Andrews, 1867, cited with characteristic modern disapproval by Jespersen, *The Philosophy of Grammar*, London, Allen and Unwin, 1924, p. 47).

Another and rather different development of the view that language (in its deeper structure) mirrors thought can be found in the work of Frege, Russell, and the early Wittgenstein. This is well known, and I will not discuss it further here.

60. N. Beauzée, *Grammaire générale, ou exposition raisonnée des éléments nécessaires du langage* (1767). Page references here and below are to the revised and corrected edition of 1819.

61. This of course leaves quite open the question of how creative thought is possible, and the discussion of this matter was no more satisfactory than any account that can be given today—that is, it is left as a complete mystery. Cordemoy, for example, attributes "les nouvelles pensées qui nous viennent, sans que nous en puissions trouver la cause en nous-mesmes, n'y l'attribuer à l'entretien des hommes" to "inspiration," that is, to communication from disembodied spirits (*op. cit.*, pp. 185–186). Many others of the period would agree that, in some way or other, "man possesses some analogy to the Divine attributes in his intellectual faculties" (Herbert of Cherbury, *De Veritate*, 1624, p. 167; page references here and below are to the translation by M. H. Carré, University of Bristol Studies No. 6, 1937). This invocation of the super-

natural should be considered against the background of the revived neo-Platonism, with its interpretation of human creativity
as an analogue of divine "emanation," in aesthetic theory from
the sixteenth century through romanticism. For discussion, see
Lovejoy, Abrams (*op. cit.*), and further references given there.

62. Recall that for La Mettrie the soul is not a separate substance;
rather, "since all the faculties of the soul depend to such a degree
on the proper organization of the brain and of the whole body,
that apparently they are but this organization itself, the soul is
clearly an enlightened machine"; "the soul is therefore but an
empty word, of which no one has any idea, and which an enlightened man should use only to signify the part in us that
thinks" (p. 128). He admits forthrightly, regarding the "imaginative faculty" of the brain, that its "nature is as unknown to us
as its way of acting" and that its products are "the marvelous
and incomprehensible result of the structure of the brain" (p.
107). Later writers are much less diffident and describe the brain
as secreting thought much as the liver secretes bile (Cabanis),
and so on.

63. The Cartesians characteristically assumed that mental processes
are common to all normal humans and that languages may therefore differ in the manner of expression but not in the thoughts
expressed. Cordemoy, for example, in discussing language learning (*op. cit.*, pp. 40ff.; cf. p. 63, below), describes the acquisition of a second language as merely a matter of assigning new
linguistic expressions to the ideas that are already associated with
expressions of the first language. It follows, then, that there should
be no fundamental difficulty in translating from one language
to another. This claim, of course, would be vigorously denied
by the romantics, who think of language not just as a "mirror
of the mind" but as a constitutive element in mental processes
and as a reflection of cultural individuality (cf. Herder: "Der
schönste Versuch über die Geschichte und mannigfaltige Charak-
teristik des menschlichen Verstandes und Herzens wäre also eine
philosophische Vergleichung der Sprachen; denn in jede dersel-
ben ist der Verstand eines Volkes und sein Charakter geprägt,"
Ideen zur Philosophie der Geschichte der Menschheit, 1784–1785,
in Heintel, *op. cit.*, p. 176).

64. We return to some of its concrete proposals directly.

65. Page references are to *Works*, vol. I (cf. note 28).

66. It follows, then, that the interrogative and indicative (in which

the response is made) are closely related. "So near indeed is this Affinity, that in these two Modes alone the Verb retains the same Form, nor are they otherwise distinguished, than either by the Addition or Absence of some small particle, or by some minute change in the collocation of the words, or sometimes only by a change in the Tone, or Accent" (p. 299). More precisely, in the case of a "simple interrogative" (i.e., a simple yes-or-no question), the response is (except for possible ellipsis) made in almost the same words as the interrogative; "indefinite interrogatives," however, "may be answered by infinite affirmatives, and infinite negatives. For instance—*Whose are these Verses?* We may answer affirmatively—*They are* Virgil's, *They are* Horace's, *They are* Ovid's, etc.—or negatively—*They are not* Virgil's, *They are not* Horace's, *They are not* Ovid's, and so one, either way, to infinity" (p. 300, footnote).

67. Apart from its Cartesian origins, the Port-Royal theory of language, with its distinction between deep and surface structure, can be traced to scholastic and renaissance grammar; in particular, to the theory of ellipsis and "ideal types" that reached its fullest development in Sanctius's *Minerva* (1587). For some discussion, see Sahlin, *op. cit.*, chap. 1 and pp. 89f.

68. This transformation is not mentioned, but it is implicit in the examples that are given.

69. Arnauld, *La Logique, ou l'art de penser* (1662). Translated by J. Dickoff and P. James as *The Art of Thinking*, Bobbs-Merrill (1964). Pages references are to this translation. For some recent discussion of the linguistic significance of this work, see H. E. Brekle, "Semiotik und linguistische Semantik in Port-Royal," *Indogermanische Forschungen*, vol. 69, pp. 103–121 (1964).

70. The notion "idea" in Cartesian thought is crucial but difficult. Several terms are used (e.g., "idea," "notion") apparently without a systematic distinction in sense, and the concept itself is not clearly characterized. In the *Meditations*, III, Descartes relates the term "idea" to "image," stating that "of my thoughts some are, so to speak, images of the things, and to these alone is the title 'idea' [Latin: *idea*] properly applied" (Haldane and Ross, vol. 1, p. 59; of course, these "images" may be derived by imagination or reflection, rather than received through sense). In his reply to Hobbes's *Objection* to this passage, Descartes clarifies his intentions (modifying his formulation in the process, so it appears) stating that "I take the term 'idea' to stand for whatever

the mind directly perceives; and so when I will or when I fear, since at the same time I perceive that I will and fear, that very volition and apprehension are ranked among my ideas (Haldane and Ross, vol. II, pp. 67–68). The latter use of "idea" as, essentially, an object of thought, is the one that seems consistent with his general usage. For example, in the *Discourse on Method* he speaks of "certain laws which God has so established in Nature, and of which He has imprinted such ideas [French: *notions*] on our minds" (Haldane and Ross, vol. I, p. 106). Similarly, in the *Principles of Philosophy* (*op. cit.*, p. 224), no fundamental distinction is made between "the ideas [Latin: *ideas*] of number and figure" and other "ordinary conceptions [Latin: *notiones*] of the mind, for example, that 'if *equals are added to equals, the result is equal,*' and so on" (part I, principle XIII). The latter usage of the term "idea," as anything that can be "conceived" (not merely "imagined"), is the one carried over to the Port-Royal *Logic*. In this sense, concepts of varied types, even propositions are ideas. This usage is widespread. Lamy (*op. cit.*, p. 7), who makes no pretense to originality, describes ideas as "les objets de nos perceptions" and asserts that "outre ces idées qui sont excitées par ce qui touche nostre corps, nous en trouvons d'autres dans le fond de nostre nature, qui n'entrent point dans nostre esprit par les sens, comme sont celles qui nous representent les premieres veritez: Par exemple celles-cy, Qu'il faut rendre à chacun ce qui luy appartient: qu'il est impossible qu'une chose soit, et qu'elle ne soit pas en un même-temps, etc." In general, the discussion of simple and complex propositions throughout the Port-Royal *Grammar* and *Logic* suggests this concept of "idea," since propositions are described as formed by combining ideas, and complex ideas are described as based on underlying constituent propositions. In this sense, "idea" is a theoretical term of the theory of mental processes; the comprehension (i.e., intension or meaning) of an idea is the fundamental notion in semantic interpretation, and in so far as the deep structure of language is regarded as a direct reflection of mental processes, it is the fundamental notion in the analysis of thought.

For further discussion see J. Veitch, *The Method, Meditations, and Selections from the Principles of Descartes*, Edinburgh, Blackwood and Sons (1880), note II, pp. 276–285.

71. In the French original, the cited sentence is: *La doctrine qui met le souverain bien dans la volupté du corps, laquelle a été en-*

seignée par Epicure, est indigne d'un Philosophe. The Dickoff-
James translation, which I have followed elsewhere, translates
this as: *The doctrine which identifies the sovereign good with
the sensual pleasure of the body and which was taught by Epicurus is unworthy of a philosopher.* But in this translation the
explicative relative *which was taught by Epicurus* would naturally be taken as a determinative clause conjoined with the first
determinative clause *which identifies* . . ., in which case the point
of the example is lost.

72. Notice, incidentally, that adjective-noun constructions in the
surface structure may derive by grammatical transformations of
the type proposed in the Port-Royal *Grammar* from either type
of relative, as is evident from the examples given there and, more
strikingly, in such ambiguous examples as Jespersen's *The indus-
trious Japanese will conquer in the long run* (*op. cit.*, p. 112).

73. Notice that, in such cases, it is not true that each of the elementary abstract objects constituting the deep structure itself underlies a possible sentence; thus *je vous dis*, for example, is not a
sentence in itself. In current terminology, it is not the case that
each item generated by the underlying base (phrase structure)
rules underlies a possible kernel sentence. Similarly, in all work
in transformational generative grammar of the last ten years or
more, it has been taken for granted that the phrase-structure
rules can introduce "dummy symbols" that receive a representation in terms of morpheme strings only as a result of application
of embedding rules of one sort or another (as, for example, in
verb-complement constructions in English), and the elementary
strings in which these dummy symbols appear will not underlie
kernel sentences. Various related ideas that have been explored
during this period are summarized and discussed in Chomsky,
Aspects of the Theory of Syntax, chap. III.

74. A rather different analysis of these structures is presented by
Beauzée, *op. cit.* He regards them as based on relative clauses
with the antecedent transformationally deleted. Thus the sentences *l'état présent des Juifs prouve que notre religion est divine,
ich glaube dass ich liebe, I think (that) I love*, derive, respectively,
from *l'état présent des Juifs prouve une vérité qui est, notre religion est divine, Ich glaube ein Ding dass ist, ich liebe, I think a
thing that is, I love* (p. 405).

75. For further discussion, see Chomsky, *Aspects of the Theory of
Syntax*. It is worth mentioning that the theory of transforma-

tional generative grammar has in many respects moved toward a point of view like that implicit in the Port-Royal theory, as new evidence and insights have accumulated during the few years in which it has, once again, become an object of fairly intensive investigation.

76. Some earlier notions are reviewed by Sahlin, *op. cit.*, pp. 97f. The idea that a sentence can be regarded simply as a sequence of words or word categories, with no further structure, is frequently expressed (whether or not it is actually believed) by many later writers.

77. Notice that this is referred to as the principal, not the unique role of verbs. They are also used "pour signifier d'autres mouvemens de nostre ame; comme desirer, prier, commander, etc." (p. 90). These matters are taken up again in chap. XV, where the grammatical means by which these mental states and processes are realized in various languages are briefly discussed. See p. 41, above.

78. The *Grammar* goes on to observe that it would be a mistake to assume, with certain earlier grammarians, that verbs necessarily express actions or passions or something that is taking place, and it offers as counterexamples such verbs as *existit, quiescit, friget, alget, tepet, calet, albet, viret, claret* (p. 94).

79. As noted earlier (p. 117): "it is often necessary to transform such a sentence from the active to the passive voice in order to put the argument into its most natural form and to express explicitly that which is to be proved."

80. It is hardly just to attribute this insight to twentieth-century British philosophy, as its "central and fundamental discovery" (cf. Flew, *Introduction to Logic and Language*, First series, Oxford, Blackwell, 1952, p. 7; or Wittgenstein, *Tractatus Logico-Philosophicus*, 1922, 4.0031, where it is attributed to Russell). Nor is the observation that "grammatical resemblances and dissimilarities may be logically misleading" (Flew, p. 8) quite as novel an insight as Flew suggests. See, for example, p. 50, below.

The general assumption of Cartesian linguistics is that the surface organization of a sentence may not give a true and full representation of the grammatical relations that play a role in determining its semantic content, and, as we have noted, a theory of grammar is sketched in which actual sentences are derived from underlying "deep structures" in which these relations are grammatically represented. The extent to which "logical form" is actually represented by the syntactically defined deep structures, in the technical modern sense or the related sense suggested in Cartesian linguistics, is a further and in many respects open question. See J. Katz, *The Philosophy of Language*, Harper & Row (1966), for discussion.

81. Referred to, typically, as the "ordre naturel." See p. 28, above.

82. Many of Du Marsais's published and unpublished works on language are printed posthumously in *Logique et Principes de Grammaire* (1769). Page references here are to this volume. The correlation between freedom of word order and inflection is noted by many other writers, e.g., Adam Smith in his *Considerations concerning the First Formation of Languages*.

83. When Bloomfield (along with many others) criticizes premodern linguistics for obscuring the structural difference between languages "by forcing their descriptions into the scheme of Latin grammar" (*Language*, p. 8), he is presumably referring to such claims as this, which he regards as having been disproven. If so, then it must be observed that his book contains no evidence to support either the conclusion that philosophical grammar was wedded to a Latin model, or the conclusion that its actual hypothesis concerning the uniformity of underlying grammatical relations has been brought into question by modern work.

In general, it should be noted that Bloomfield's account of premodern linguistics is not reliable. His historical survey consists of a few haphazard remarks that, he asserts, summarize "what eighteenth century scholars knew about language." These remarks are not always accurate (as, for example, his astonishing assertion that prior to the nineteenth century linguists "had not observed the sounds of speech, and confused them with the written symbols of the alphabet" or that the writers of general grammars regarded Latin as supreme in embodying the "universal canons of logic"); and, where accurate, they give little indication of the character of what was done in this period.

The manner in which the sounds of speech were analyzed in this period deserves a separate discussion; it is quite arbitrary to exclude this topic from the present survey, as I have done. Most of the works discussed here, and many others, contain discussions of phonetics, and the Aristotelian dictum that "spoken words are the symbols of mental experience and written words are the symbols of spoken words" (*De Interpretatione*, 1) is apparently accepted with no discussion. There are a few modern references to the phonetics of this period. For example, M Grammont comments on the phonetics in Cordemoy, *op. cit.*, in the following terms: "... les articulations d'un certain nombre de phonèmes français sont décrites avec une netteté et une exactitude remarquables" (*Traité de phonétique*, Paris, Librairie Delagrave, 1933, 4th ed., 1950, p. 13n.; he goes on to observe that: "Ce sont ces descriptions que Molière a reproduites mot pour mot dans *Le Bourgeois gentilhomme*, acte II, scène 6 (1670)").

84. *Op. cit.*, pp. 340f. Bentham suggests a similar analysis (*op. cit.*, p. 356).

85. A distinction between the "ideas principally expressed" by a linguistic form and the "accessory ideas" associated with it is developed in the Port-Royal *Logic*, chaps. 14, 15. The principal idea is what is stated by the "lexical definition," which attempts to formulate in a precise way the "truth of usage." But the lexical definition cannot "reflect the whole impression the defined word makes on the mind," and "it often happens that a word excites in our minds, besides the principal idea which we regard as the proper meaning of the word, other ideas—ideas which we may call accessory ideas and to which though we receive their impression we do not explicitly attend" (p. 90). For example, the principal meaning of *you lied* is that you knew that the opposite of what you said is true. "But in addition to this principal meaning, these words convey an idea of contempt and outrage which suggest that the speaker would not hesitate to harm you—a suggestion which renders his words both offensive and injurious." Similarly, Virgil's line *To die, is that such a wretched thing?* (*Usque adeone mori miserum est?*) has the same principal meaning as *It is not so very wretched to die* (*Non est usque adeo mori miserum*), but the original "expresses not only the bare thought that death is not so bad a thing as one supposes but suggests as well the image of a man who challenges death and looks it fearless in the face" (pp. 91–92). Accessory ideas may be "permanently attached to words," as in the cases just mentioned, or they may be attached only in a particular utterance, for example, by gesture or tone of voice (p. 90). The association may, in other words, be a matter either of *langue* or *parole*.

The distinction is rather like that of cognitive and emotive meaning. Also relevant to contemporary issues is the example (p. 91) of how certain grammatical processes may change the accessory ideas expressed, without modification of principal meaning; thus, so it is claimed, to accuse someone of ignorance or deceit is different from calling him ignorant and deceitful, since the adjectival forms "express, in addition to the idea of particular shortcomings, an idea of contempt, whereas the nouns mean only the particular lack with no accompanying condemnation."

86. C. Buffier, *Grammaire françoise sur un plan nouveau* (1709), cited by Sahlin, *op. cit.*, pp. 121–122, with typical modern disparagement based, once again, on the assumption that surface structure alone is a proper object of study. See J. Katz and P. Postal, *An Integrated Theory of Linguistic Descriptions*, §§4.2.3, 4.2.4, for development and justification of a very similar idea.

87. "De la construction grammaticale," *op. cit.*, p. 229.

88. The Latin example suggests a variety of problems, however. For some remarks on the phenomenon of so-called "free word order," within the present context, see Chomsky, *Aspects of the Theory of Syntax*, chap. 2, §4.4.

89. It is not entirely clear from the context whether these conditions on transformations are regarded as matters of *langue* or *parole*, as conditions on a grammar or on the usage of a grammar; nor is it clear whether, within the framework that Du Marsais accepts, this question can be sensibly raised.

The account of sentence interpretation given by Du Marsais can be profitably compared with that proposed by Katz, Fodor, and Postal in recent work. See Katz and Postal, *op. cit.*, and references cited there.

90. The examples that I give here are cited by Sahlin as indicative of the ridiculous character of Du Marsais's theory, concerning which: "il serait injuste de la confronter avec la science moderne pour y relever des erreurs trops évidentes" (Sahlin, *op. cit.*, p. 84).

91. T. Reid, *Essays on the Intellectual Powers of Man* (1785). For some remarks and quotations, see Chomsky, *Aspects of the Theory of Syntax*, pp. 199–200.

92. Except to the extent indicated by the final example, the analysis of indefinite articles. Such attempts to go beyond surface form are tolerated by modern linguistic theory and have been the subject of much methodological discussion, particularly, in the United States during the 1940s.

93. See Postal, *Constituent Structure*, The Hague, Mouton (1964), for discussion of contemporary approaches to syntax that accept

this limitation. Many modern methodological discussions actually imply, further, that linguistic investigation should be restricted to the surface structure of the given utterances of a fixed corpus; thus Sahlin reflects modern attitudes in criticizing Du Marsais (p. 36) for the "défaut inexcusable chez un grammarien" of using invented examples instead of restricting himself to utterances actually observed in living speech, as though a rational alternative were conceivable.

For further discussion of the problem of analyzing deep and surface structure see Chomsky, *Syntactic Structures*, The Hague, Mouton (1957), *Current Issues in Linguistic Theory, Aspects of the Theory of Syntax;* Lees, *Grammar of English Nominalizations*, The Hague, Mouton (1960); Postal, "Underlying and Superficial Linguistic Structures," *Harvard Educational Review*, 34 (1964); Katz and Postal, *An Integrated Theory of Linguistic Descriptions;* Katz, *The Philosophy of Language;* and many other publications.

94. To mention just one example, consider Harnois's introductory statement in his discussion of "philosophical grammar" (*op. cit.*, p. 18; it should be emphasized that this discussion is unusual in that it at least pays attention to the actual doctrines that were held by philosophical grammarians, instead of attributing to them absurd beliefs that were completely counter to their actual work). He points out that participants in this work felt themselves to be contributing "à une science qui avait déjà produit une oeuvre fondamentale [viz., the Port-Royal *Grammar*], c'est-à-dire d'enricher un patrimoine existant et d'augmenter le nombre des résultats déjà acquis. Cette croyance peut paraître ridicule à un linguiste moderne, mais elle était réelle."

It should be mentioned that the modern disparagement of traditional linguistic theory develops, not only from the decision to restrict attention to surface structure, but also, quite often, from the uncritical acceptance of a "behaviorist" account of language use and acquisition, common in its essentials to several fields—an account that seems to me to be pure mythology.

95. *Véritables principes de la grammaire* (1729), quoted by Sahlin, *op. cit.*, pp. 29-30. The dating of this is discussed by Sahlin in the Introduction, p. ix. Much earlier, Arnauld had pointed out that "on n'a pas accoutumé de traiter dans les Grammaires particulières ce qui est commun à toutes les langues" (1669, cited by Sainte-Beuve, *op. cit.*, p. 538), and the distinction between

general and particular grammar is implicit, though not expressed, in the Port-Royal *Grammar*. Wilkins also distinguishes between "natural" (that is, "philosophical," "rational," or "universal") grammar, which deals with the "ground and rules as do necessarily belong to philosophy of letters and speech," and "instituted" or "particular" grammar, which deals with the "rules which are particular to a given language" (*op. cit.*, p. 297).

96. Beauzée, *op. cit.*, Preface, pp. v–vi.

97. Quoted by Sahlin, *op. cit.*, p. 21. Note that there is a difference in emphasis in the remarks of Beauzée and D'Alembert on the relation between particular facts and general principles. The two views, however, are not inconsistent.

98. Cf. Sainte-Beuve, *op. cit.*, pp. 538f.; Harnois, *op. cit.*, p. 20.

99. There is, to be sure, an implicit element of so-called "prescriptivism" in his choice of "cultivated usage" (that is, the usage of the best authors, but, particularly, "l'usage de la parole prononcée" in the Court) as the object of description.

100. Note that a restriction of linguistic study to description without explanation does not entail a corresponding restriction to the investigation of surface structure. The latter is a further and independent limitation.

101. Vaugelas is by no means the first to insist on the primacy of usage. A century before, in one of the earliest French grammars, Meigret insists that "nous devons dire comme nous disons" and that one may not "prescrire aucune loi contre l'usage de la prononciation française" (quoted by Ch.-L. Livet, *La grammaire française et les grammariens du XVIᵉ siècle*).

It is interesting to note that the reaction of the Cartesian linguists against pure descriptivism recapitulates the evolution of speculative grammar in the thirteenth century, as an attempt to provide rational explanation in place of a mere record of usage. Speculative grammar also distinguished universal from particular grammar; for example, Roger Bacon assumes that "with respect to its *substance* grammar is one and the same in all languages, although it does vary *accidentally* (*Grammatica Graeca*, edited by Charles, p. 278, cited in N. Kretzmann, "History of Semantics," in *Encyclopedia of Philosophy*, edited by P. Edwards, forthcoming).

102. Quoted by Sahlin, *op. cit.*, p. 26, from the article "Datif" in the *Encyclopedia*. Sahlin also gives (p. 45) a much earlier quote from the *Véritables principes* (see note 95): "La grammaire

n'est pas avant les langues. Il n'y a point de langue qui ait été faite sur la grammaire; les observations des grammairiens doivent être faites sur l'usage, et ne sont point des lois qui l'aient précédé." This quote is followed by the comment that Du Marsais did not adhere to this principle, but, though there is much to criticize in his work, I find little evidence to support this charge.

103. This is, of course, consistent with Cartesian methodology, which insists on the necessity of observation and of crucial experiment for choice among competing explanations. See the *Discourse on Method*, part VI. The Cartesian origins of the concern for a "grammaire générale" (expressing what is a common human possession) and a "grammaire raisonnée" (which will explain facts instead of merely listing them) are too obvious to require discussion. Similarly, it was the newly rediscovered Aristotelian concept of rational science that led to the speculative grammar of the thirteenth century. Cf. Kretzmann, *op. cit.*

104. This discussion is due to Arnauld and appears in his correspondence a year before the publication of the *Grammar*. Cf. Sainte-Beuve, *op. cit.*, pp. 536f.

The *Grammar* is, incidentally, not entirely fair to Vaugelas in tacitly implying that he was unaware of counterexamples. In fact, Vaugelas himself mentions one of the cited counterexamples (namely, the vocative, for which he proposes an understood, deleted article). Furthermore, Vaugelas does in fact offer a tentative explanation, rather apologetically, to be sure, for the rule as he formulates it.

105. For further discussion of the matter of explanation in linguistics, see Chomsky, *Syntactic Structures;* "Explanatory Models in Linguistics," in E. Nagel, P. Suppes, A. Tarski (eds.), *Logic, Methodology and Philosophy of Science*, Stanford University Press (1962); *Current Issues in Linguistic Theory;* Katz, "Mentalism in Linguistics," *Language*, vol. 40, pp. 124–137 (1964).

One of the most striking features of American descriptivism in the 1940s was its insistence on justification in terms of precisely specified procedures of analysis. The emphasis on precision and on the necessity for justification of descriptive statements in some language-independent terms constitutes a major contribution. But the requirements that were placed on justification (namely, that it be "procedural," in the sense of the methodological discussions of the 1940s) were so strong as to make the enterprise unfeasible, and some of the reactions to this stringency (in particular, the view that any clearly specified procedure of analysis is as good as any other) detracted substantially from its potential significance.

106. Observe, however, that the discussion in the Port-Royal *Grammar*, if interpreted quite literally, does not identify the underlying structures with actual sentences. Cf. p. 39, above, and note 73. It is thus quite close, in conception, to transformational generative grammar of the sort developed in the references of note 93, which has also been based on the assumption that the structures to which transformational rules apply are abstract underlying forms, not actual sentences. Notice, incidentally, that the theory of transformations as originally developed by Harris, outside of the framework of generative grammar, does regard transformations as relations among actual sentences and is, in fact, much closer to the conception of Du Marsais and others, in this respect (see Z. S. Harris, "Co-occurrence and Transformation in Linguistic Structure," *Language*, vol. 33, pp. 283-340, 1957, and many other references). See Chomsky, *Current Issues in Linguistic Theory*, p. 62n., for some discussion bearing on this point.

107. Humboldt's picture was, however, a good bit more complex. Cf. pp. 19–28, above.

108. Notice that, when described in these terms, linguistic universals need not be found in every language. Thus, for example, when a certain set of phonetic features is claimed to constitute a universal phonetics, it is not proposed that each of these features functions in every language, but rather that every language makes its particular choice from among this system of features. Cf. Beauzée, *op. cit.*, p. ix: "les *Éléments nécessaires du Langage* . . . sont en effet dans toutes les langues, d'une nécessité indispensable pour rendre sensible l'exposition analytique et métaphysique de la pensée. Mais je ne prétends point parler d'une nécessité individuelle, qui ne laisse à aucun idiome la liberté d'en rejeter aucun; je veux seulement marquer une nécessité d'espèce, qui fixe les bornes du choix que l'on peut en faire."

109. Translated by M. H. Carré (1937), University of Bristol Studies, No. 6.

110. These developments are familiar except, perhaps, for seventeenth-century English Platonism. See A. O. Lovejoy, "Kant and the English Platonists," in *Essays Philosophical and Psychological in Honor of William James*, New York, Longmans, Green and Co.

(1908), for some discussion of English Platonism, in particular, of its interest in the "ideas and categories which enter into every presentation of objects and make possible the unity and interconnectedness of rational experience." Lovejoy's account, in turn, is based heavily on G. Lyons, *L'idéalisme en Angleterre au XVIIIᵉ siècle*, Paris (1888). See also J. Passmore, *Ralph Cudworth*, Cambridge University Press (1951); L. Gysi, *Platonism and Cartesianism in the Philosophy of Ralph Cudworth*, Bern, Verlag Herbert Lang and Cie. (1962). Some relevant quotes from Descartes, Leibniz, and others are given in Chomsky, *Aspects of the Theory of Syntax*, chap. 1, §8, where the relevance of this position to current issues is also briefly discussed.

See also Chomsky, *Explanatory Models in Linguistics*, and Katz, *Philosophy of Language*, for discussion of an essentially rationalist approach to the problem of language acquisition and of the inadequacy of empiricist alternatives. In the same connection, see Lenneberg, *op. cit.* and *The Biological Bases for Language* (John Wiley, forthcoming), and §VI of J. Fodor and J. Katz (eds.), *The Structure of Language: Readings in the Philosophy of Language*, Englewood Cliffs, N.J., Prentice-Hall (1964).

111. Leibniz, *Discourse on Metaphysics*. The quotations here are from the English translation by G. R. Montgomery, La Salle, Illinois, Open Court (1902). With reference to Plato's theory, Leibniz insists only that it be "purged of the error of preexistence." Similarly, Cudworth accepts the theory of reminiscence without the doctrine of preexistence that Plato suggests as an explanation for the facts he describes: "And this is the only true and allowable sense of that old assertion, that knowledge is reminiscence; not that it is the rememberance of something which the soul had some time before actually known in a pre-existent state, but because it is the mind's comprehending of things by some inward anticipations of its own, something native and domestic to it, or something actively exerted from within itself" (*Treatise concerning Eternal and Immutable Morality*, p. 424; page references, here and below, are to the first American edition of works of Cudworth, vol. II, T. Birch, ed., 1838).

Leibniz's view (*Discourse on Metaphysics*, §26) that "the mind at every moment expresses all its future thoughts and already thinks confusedly of all that of which it will ever think distinctly" might be regarded as suggesting the fundamental insight regarding language (and thought) that we discussed in §2.

112. Cf. Beauzée, *op. cit.*, pp. xv–xvi. He defines "la Métaphysique grammaticale" as being nothing but "la nature du Langage mise à découvert, constatée par ses propres faits, et réduite à des notions générales":

> Les finesses que cette Métaphysique découvre dans le Langage . . . viennent de la raison éternelle, qui nous dirige à notre insu. . . . Vainement prétendroit-on que ceux qui parlent le mieux n'aperçoivent pas ces principes délicats. Comment pourroient-ils les mettre si supérieurement en pratique sans les apercevoir en aucune façon? J'avoue qu'ils ne seroient peut-être pas en état d'en raisonner sur-le-champ selon toutes les régles, parce qu'ils n'en ont point étudié l'ensemble et le système; mais enfin, puisqu'ils suivent ces principes, il les sentent donc au-dedans d'eux-mêmes; ils ne peuvent se dérober aux impressions de cette Logique naturelle qui dirige secrètement, mais irrésistiblement, les esprits droits dans toutes leurs opérations. Or la Grammaire générale n'est que l'exposition raisonnée des procédés de cette Logique naturelle.

113. But cf. p. 58, above. The typical Cartesian view would apparently have been that, although these principles may function unconsciously, they can be brought to consciousness by introspection.

114.   Mais quelque peine qu'on se donne pour leur apprendre certaines choses, on s'apperçoit souvent qu'ils sçavent les noms de mille autres choses qu'on n'a point eu dessein de leur montrer; et ce qu'il y a de plus surprenant en cela, c'est de voir lorsqu'ils ont deux ou trois ans, que par la seule force de leur attention, ils soient capables de demesler dans toutes les constructions qu'on fait en parlant d'une mesme chose, le nom qu'on donne à cette chose (p. 47–48).

He also points out that children learn their native language more easily than an adult can learn a new language.

It is interesting to compare these quite commonplace but perfectly correct observations with the picture of language learning that one generally finds among many modern writers, whose conclusions are, in fact, based not on observation but on a priori assumptions about what they believe must take place. Cf., e.g., the speculation on how all language "habits" are built up by training, instruction, conditioning, and reinforcement in Bloomfield, *op. cit.*, pp. 29–31; Wittgenstein, *Blue Book* (Blackwell, 1958), pp. 1, 12–13, 77; Skinner, *Verbal Behavior* (New York, Appleton-Century-Crofts, 1957); Quine, *Word and Object* (M.I.T., Wiley, 1960); etc.

Occasionally, modern discussions invoke some process of "generalization" or "abstraction" that functions along with association and conditioning, but it must be emphasized that there is no known process of this sort that will begin to overcome the inadequacy of empiricist accounts of language acquisition. For discussion, see the references of note 110. In considering this problem, one must, in particular, bear in mind the criticism advanced by Cudworth (*op. cit.*, p. 462) against the attempt to show how general ideas might arise from sensory images (phantasms) by "abstraction" and thus require no postulation of innate mental structure. As he points out, the *intellectus agens* either "doth know what he is to do with these phantasms beforehand, what he is to make of them, and unto what shape to bring them," in which case the question is begged, an "intelligible idea" being presupposed; or, if he has no such plan, "he must needs be a bungling workman," that is, the act of "abstracting" can lead to any arbitrary and absurd result.

In short, reference to "generalization" does not eliminate the necessity to provide a precise account of the basis on which acquisition of beliefs and knowledge proceeds. We may, if we like, refer to the processes involved in language acquisition as processes of generalization or abstraction. But we will then apparently be forced to conclude that "generalization" or "abstraction," in this new sense, has no recognizable relation to what is called "generalization" or "abstraction" in any technical or well-defined usage of philosophy, psychology, or linguistics.

115. Cf. Steinthal, *Gedächtnissrede*, p. 17. He holds that Humboldt's fundamental insight was to see "wie nichts von aussen in den Menschen kommen könnte, wenn es nicht ursprünglich in ihm läge, und wie aller Einfluss von aussen nur ein Reiz für das Hervorbrechen des Innern ist. In der Tiefe dieses Innern liegt der einheitliche Quell aller echten Dichtung und echten Philosophie, der Quell aller Ideen und aller grossen menschheitlichen Schöpfungen; und aus ihm fliesst auch die Sprache."

Humboldt's views on education, incidentally, illustrate the same concern for the creative role of the individual. In his early essay against state absolutism (see p. 24f., above), he argues that "sound instruction undoubtedly consists of spreading out before the person to be instructed various solutions, and then preparing him to choose the most appropriate, or even better, to invent his own solution by simply arranging before him all the difficulties to be conquered." This method of instruction is, he maintains, not available to the state, which is limited to coercive and authoritarian means. Cf. Cowan, *op. cit.*, p. 43. Elsewhere he holds that "all educational development has its sole origin in the inner psychological constitution of human beings, and can only be stimulated, never produced by external institutions" (Cowan, p. 126). "Man's understanding, like all his other energies, is cultivated only by each human being's own activity, his own inventiveness, or his own utilization of the inventions of others" (Cowan, pp. 42–43). Cf. also Cowan, pp. 132ff.

It is interesting to compare Harris's observation in his *Hermes* that there is "nothing more absurd than the common notion of Instruction, as if Science were to be poured into the Mind like water into a cistern, that passively waits to receive all that comes. The growth of knowledge . . . [rather resembles] . . . the growth of Fruit; however external causes may in some degree cooperate, it is the internal vigour, and virtue of the tree, that must ripen the juices to their just maturity" (*Works*, p. 209). Here the ideal is apparently Socratic method; as Cudworth describes it (*op. cit.*, p. 427), the belief that "knowledge was not to be poured into the soul like liquor, but rather to be invited and gently drawn forth from it; nor the mind so much to be filled therewith from without, like a vessel, as to be kindled and awaked."

116. On the relation between Cudworth and Descartes, see Passmore, *op. cit.;* Gysi, *op. cit;* and, for more general background, S. P. Lamprecht, "The Role of Descartes in Seventeenth-century England," *Studies in the History of Ideas*, vol. III, edited by the Department of Philosophy of Columbia University, Columbia University Press, pp. 181–242 (1935). Passmore concludes (*op. cit.*, p. 8) that, despite some divergence, "it is still not misleading to call Cudworth a Cartesian, so great was their agreement on so many vital issues."

117. Cf. Descartes, Meditation II, Haldane and Ross, p. 155: we know what it is that we see not "by means of vision" but "by the intuition of the mind"; "when looking from a window and saying I see men who pass in the street, I really do not see them, but infer that what I see is men."

118. However, "the cogitations that we have of corporeal things [are]

usually both noematical and phantasmatical together." This accounts for the fact that geometricians will rely on diagrams and that "in speech, metaphors and allegories do so exceedingly please" (pp. 430, 468).

119. In a similar way, Cudworth arrives at the typical rationalist conclusion that our knowledge is organized as a kind of "deductive system" by which we arrive at "a descending comprehension of a thing from the universal ideas of the mind, and not an ascending perception of them from individuals by sense" (p. 467).

120. See Abrams, *op. cit.*, for discussion of the importance of this theory of cognitive processes in romantic aesthetics, and of its origins in earlier thought, particularly, that of Plotinus, who "explicitly rejected the concept of sensations as 'imprints' or 'seal-impressions' made on a passive mind, and substituted the view of the mind as an act and a power which 'gives a radiance out of its own store' to the objects of sense" (Abrams, p. 59). Parallels between Kant and seventeenth-century English philosophy are discussed by Lovejoy, *Kant and the English Platonists*.

121. Quoted in A. D. Snyder, *Coleridge on Logic and Learning*, New Haven, Yale University Press (1929), pp. 133–134.

122. Quoted in Snyder, *op. cit.*, p. 116.

123. See, for example, D. M. MacKay, "Mindlike Behavior in Artefacts," *British Journal for Philosophy of Science*, vol. 2 (1951), pp. 105–121. J. S. Bruner, "On Perceptual Readiness," *Phychological Review*, vol. 64 (1957), pp. 123–152, "Neural Mechanisms in Perception," *Psychological Review*, vol. 64 (1957), pp. 340–358. For a review of many of the findings relating to central processes in perception, see H. L. Teuber, "Perception," in the *Handbook of Physiology–Neurophysiology* III, J. Field, H. W. Magoun, V. E. Hall (eds.), American Physiological Society, Washington, D.C., 1960), chap. LXV.

124. For discussion and references in the areas of phonology and syntax respectively, see M. Halle and K. N. Stevens, "Speech Recognition: A Model and a Program for Research," in Fodor and Katz (eds.), *op. cit.;* and G. A. Miller and N. Chomsky, "Finitary Models of Language Users," part 2, in R. D. Luce, R. Bush, and E. Galanter (eds.), *Handbook of Mathematical Psychology*, vol. II, New York, Wiley (1963).

Bibliography

Aarslef, H.: "Leibniz on Locke on Language," *American Philosophical Quarterly*, vol. 1, no. 3, pp. 1–24, 1964.

Abrams, M. H.: *The Mirror and the Lamp*, Oxford University Press, Fair Lawn, N.J., 1953.

Aristotle: *De Interpretatione*.

———: *De Anima*.

Arnauld, A.: *La Logique, ou l'art de penser*, 1662; trans. J. Dickoff and P. James as *The Art of Thinking*, The Bobbs-Merrill Company, Inc., Indianapolis, 1964.

Bacon, R.: *Grammatica Graeca*.

Bayle, F.: *The General System of the Cartesian Philosophy*, 1669; English trans., 1670.

Bayle, P.: *Historical and Critical Dictionary*, 1697; selections trans. R. H. Popkin, The Bobbs-Merrill Company, Inc., Indianapolis, 1965.

Beauzée, N.: Grammaire générale, ou exposition raisonnée des éléments nécessaires du language, 1767; rev. ed., 1819.

Bentham, J.: *Works*, ed. J. Bowring, Russell and Russell, Inc., New York, 1962.

Berthelot, R.: *Science et philosophie chez Goethe*, F. Alcan, Paris, 1932.

Bloomfield, L.: *Language*, Holt, Rinehart and Winston, Inc., New York, 1933.

Bougeant, Père G. H.: *Amusement philosophique sur le langage des bestes*, 1739.

Brekle, H. E.: "Semiotik und linguistische Semantik in Port-Royal," *Indogermanische Forschungen*, vol. 69, pp. 103–121, 1964.

Brown, R. L.: "Some Sources and Aspects of Wilhelm von Humboldt's Conception of Linguistic Relativity," unpublished doctoral dissertation, University of Illinois, 1964.

Bruner, J. S.: "On Perceptual Readiness," *Psychological Review*, vol. 64, 1957.

Brunot, F.: *Histoire de la langue française*, Librairie Armand Colin, Paris, 1924.

Buffier, C.: *Grammaire françoise sur un plan nouveau,* 1709.

Cassirer, E.: *The Philosophy of Symbolic Forms,* 1923; English trans., Yale University Press, New Haven, Conn., 1953.

Carmichael, L.: "The Early Growth of Language Capacity in the Individual," in E. H. Lenneberg (ed.), *New Directions in the Study of Language,* The M.I.T. Press, Cambridge, Mass., 1964.

Chomsky, N.: *Syntactic Structures,* Mouton and Co., The Hague, 1957.

————: "Review of B. F. Skinner, 'Verbal Behavior,'" *Language,* vol. 35, pp. 26–58, 1959; reprinted in J. A. Fodor and J. J. Katz (eds.), *The Structure of Language,* Prentice-Hall, Inc., Englewood Cliffs, N.J., 1964.

————: "Explanatory Models in Linguistics," in E. Nagel et al. (eds.), *Logic, Methodology, and Philosophy of Science,* Stanford University Press, Stanford, Calif., 1962.

————: *Current Issues in Linguistic Theory,* Mouton and Co., The Hague, 1964; reprinted in part in Fodor and Katz, *The Structure of Language.*

————: *Aspects of the Theory of Syntax,* The M.I.T. Press, Cambridge, Mass., 1965.

Coleridge, S. T.: "Lectures and Notes of 1818," in T. Ashe (ed.), *Lectures and Notes on Shakespeare and Other English Poets,* G. Bell & Sons, Ltd., London, 1893.

Cordemoy, Géraud de: *Discours Physique de la Parole,* 1666; 2d ed., 1677; English trans., 1668.

Couturat, L., and L. Leau: *Histoire de la langue universelle,* Paris, 1903.

Cowan, M.: *Humanist without Portfolio,* Wayne State University Press, Detroit, 1963.

Cudworth, R.: *Treatise concerning Eternal and Immutable Morality,* American ed. of *Works,* ed. T. Birch, 1838.

D'Alembert, J.: *Éloge de du Marsais.*

Descartes, R.: *The Philosophical Works of Descartes,* trans. E. S. Haldane and G. R. T. Ross, Dover Publications, Inc., New York, 1955.

————: "Correspondence," trans. L. C. Rosenfield (L. Cohen), *Annals of Science,* vol. 1, no. 1, 1936.

————: "Correspondence," trans. H. A. P. Torrey, *The Philosophy of Descartes,* Holt, Rinehart and Winston, Inc., New York, 1892.

Diderot, D.: *Lettre sur les sourds et muets,* 1751.

Du Marsais, César Chesneau: *Véritables Principes de la grammaire,* 1729.

————: *Logiques et Principes de Grammaire,* 1769.

Fiesel, E.: *Die Sprachphilosophie der deutschen Romantik*, Verlag von J. C. B. Mohr, Tübingen, 1927.

Flew, A.: *Introduction to Logic and Language, First Series*, Blackwell, Oxford, 1952.

Fodor, J. A.: "Could Meaning Be an 'r$_m$'?" *Journal of Verbal Learning and Verbal Behavior*, vol. 4, pp. 73–81, 1965.

———: *Psychological Explanation*, chap. 1, "Is Psychology Possible?" Random House, Inc., New York, forthcoming.

——— and J. J. Katz: *The Structure of Language: Readings in the Philosophy of Language*, Prentice-Hall, Inc., Englewood Cliffs, N.J., 1964.

Galileo: *Dialogue on the Great World Systems*, 1630; The University of Chicago Press, Chicago, 1953.

Grammont, M.: "Review of A. Gregoire, 'Petit traité de linguistique,'" *Revue des langues romanes*, vol. 60, 1920.

———: *Traité de phonétique*, Librairie Delagrave, Paris, 1933.

Gunderson, K.: "Descartes, La Mettrie, Language and Machines," *Philosophy*, vol. 39, 1964.

Gysi, L.: *Platonism and Cartesianism in the Philosophy of Ralph Cudworth*, Verlag Herbert Lang and Cie., Bern, 1962.

Halle, M., and K. N. Stevens: "Speech Recognition: A Model and a Program for Research," in Fodor and Katz, *Structure of Language*.

Harnois, G.: "Les théories du langage en France de 1660 à 1821," *Études Françaises*, vol. 17, 1929.

Harris, J.: *Works*, ed. Earl of Malmesbury, London, 1801.

Harris, Z. S.: "Co-occurrence and Transformation in Linguistic Structure," *Language*, vol. 33, pp. 283–340, 1957; reprinted in Fodor and Katz, *Structure of Language*.

Herbert of Cherbury: *De Veritate*, 1624; trans. M. H. Carré, University of Bristol Studies No. 6, 1937.

Herder, J. G.: *Abhandlung über den Ursprung der Sprache*, 1772; reprinted in part in E. Heintel (ed.), *Herder's Sprachphilosophie*, Felix Meiner Verlag, Hamburg, 1960.

———: *Ideen zur Philosophie der Geschichte der Menschheit*, 1784–1785.

Hockett, C. F.: *A Course in Modern Linguistics*, The Macmillan Company, New York, 1958.

Huarte, J.: *Examen de Ingenios*, 1575; English trans. Bellamy, 1698.

Humboldt, Wilhelm von: *Ideen zu einem Versuch die Grenzen der Wirksamkeit des Staats zu bestimmen*, 1792; trans. in part in Cowan, *Humanist without Portfolio*, pp. 37–64.

————: *Über die Verschiedenheit des Menschlichen Sprachbaues*, 1836; facsimile ed., F. Dümmlers Verlag, Bonn, 1960.

Jespersen, O.: *The Philosophy of Grammar*, George Allen & Unwin, Ltd., London, 1924.

Joos, M. (ed.): *Readings in Linguistics*, ACLS, Washington, 1957.

Katz, J. J.: "Mentalism in Linguistics," *Language*, vol. 40, pp. 124–137, 1964.

————: *Philosophy of Language*, Harper & Row, Publishers, Incorporated, New York, 1965.

———— and P. M. Postal: *An Integrated Theory of Linguistic Description*, The M.I.T. Press, Cambridge, Mass., 1964.

Kirkinen, H.: "Les origines de la conception moderne de l'homme-machine," *Annales Academiae Scientiarum Fennicae*, Helsinki, 1961.

Kretzmann, N.: "History of Semantics," in P. Edwards (ed.), *Encyclopedia of Philosophy*, forthcoming.

La Mettrie, J. O. de: *L'Homme-Machine*, 1747; critical edition, A. Vartanian (ed.), Princeton University Press, Princeton, N.J., 1960; trans. as *Man a Machine*, The Open Court Publishing Company, La Salle, Ill., 1912.

Lamprecht, S. P.: "The Role of Descartes in Seventeenth-century England," *Studies in the History of Ideas*, vol. III, ed. Department of Philosophy, Columbia University, Columbia University Press, New York, 1935.

Lamy, B.: *De l'Art de Parler*, 1676.

Lancelot, C., and A. Arnauld: *Grammaire générale et raisonnée*, 1660.

Lees, R. B.: *Grammar of English Nominalizations*, Mouton and Co., The Hague, 1960.

Leibniz, G. W. von: *Discourse on Metaphysics*, English trans. G. R. Montgomery, The Open Court Publishing Company, La Salle, Ill., 1902.

————: *Nouveaux essais sur l'entendement humain*, trans. A. G. Langley, The Open Court Publishing Company, La Salle, Ill., 1949.

Leitzmann, A. (ed.): *Briefwechsel zwischen W. von Humboldt und A. W. Schlegel*, 1908.

Lenneberg, E. H.: "A Biological Perspective of Language," in E. H. Lenneberg (ed.), *New Directions in the Study of Language*, The M.I.T. Press, Cambridge, Mass., 1964.

————: *The Biological Bases for Language*, John Wiley & Sons, Inc., New York, forthcoming.

Livet, Ch.-L.: *La grammaire française et les grammariens du XVIe siècle*, Paris, 1859.

Lovejoy, A. O.: "Kant and the English Platonists," in *Essays Philosophical and Psychological in Honor of William James*, Longmans, Green & Co., Inc., New York, 1908.

———: *The Great Chain of Being*, Harper & Row, Publishers, Incorporated, New York, 1936.

Lyons, G.: *L'idéalisme en Angleterre au XVIIIe siècle*, Paris, 1888.

MacKay, D. M.: "Mindlike Behavior in Artefacts," *British Journal for Philosophy of Science*, vol. 2, 1951.

Magnus R.: *Goethe als Naturforscher*, Barth, Leipzig, 1906; trans. H. Norden, Abelard-Schuman, Limited, New York, 1949.

Marx, K.: *Critique of the Gotha Program*, 1875.

———: *Economic and Philosophic Manuscripts*, 1844; trans. T. B. Bottomore, in E. Fromm (ed.), *Marx's Concept of Man*, Ungar, New York, 1961.

McIntosh, Margaret M. C.: "The Phonetic and Linguistic Theory of the Royal Society School," unpublished bachelor of letters thesis, Oxford University, 1956.

Mendelsohn, E.: "The Biological Sciences in the Nineteenth Century: Some Problems and Sources," *History of Science*, vol. 3, 1964.

Mill, J. S.: *Rectorial Address at St. Andrews*, 1867.

Miller, G. A., and N. Chomsky: "Finitary Models of Language Users," in R. D. Luce et al. (eds.), *Handbook of Mathematical Psychology*, John Wiley & Sons, Inc., New York, 1963, vol. II.

Passmore, J.: *Ralph Cudworth*, Cambridge University Press, New York, 1951.

Postal, P. M.: *Constituent Structure*, Mouton and Co., The Hague, 1964.

———: "Underlying and Superficial Linguistic Structures," *Harvard Educational Review*, vol. 34, 1964.

Proudhon, P.-J.: *Correspondance*, ed. J.-A. Langlois, Librairie Internationale, Paris, 1875.

Quine, W. V. O.: *Word and Object*, John Wiley & Sons, Inc., New York, and The M.I.T. Press, Cambridge, Mass., 1960.

Reid, Thomas: *Essays on the Intellectual Powers of Man*, 1785.

Robinet, J. B.: *De la Nature*, 1761–1768.

Rocker, R.: *Nationalism and Culture*, trans. R. E. Chase, Freedom Press, London, 1937.

Rosenfield, L. C.: *From Beast-Machine to Man-Machine*, Oxford University Press, Fair Lawn, N.J., 1941.

Rousseau, Jean-Jacques: *Discourse on the Origins and Foundations of Inequality among Men*, 1755; trans. in R. D. Masters (ed.), *The First and Second Discourses*, St Martin's Press, Inc., New York, 1964.

Ryle, G.: *The Concept of Mind*, Hutchinson & Co. (Publishers), Ltd., London, 1949.

Sahlin, Gunvor: *César Chesneau du Marsais et son rôle dans l'évolution de la Grammaire générale*, Presses-Universitaires, Paris, 1928.

Sainte-Beuve, Ch.-A.: *Port Royal*, vol. III, 2d ed., Paris, 1860.

Schlegel, August Wilhelm: "Briefe über Poesie, Silbenmass und Sprache," 1795; in *Kritische Schriften und Briefe*, vol. I, *Sprache und Poetik*, W. Kohlhammer Verlag, Stuttgart, 1962.

———: *Kritische Schriften und Briefe*, vol. II, *Die Kunstlehre*, 1801, W. Kohlhammer Verlag, Stuttgart, 1963.

———: *Lectures on Dramatic Art and Literature*, 1808; trans. John Black, G. Bell & Sons, Ltd., London, 1892.

———: "De l'étymologie en général," in E. Böcking (ed.), *Oeuvres Écrites en Français*, Leipzig, 1846.

Schlegel, Friedrich von: *Geschichte der alten und neuen Literatur*, 1812.

Skinner, B. F.: *Verbal Behavior*, Appleton-Century-Crofts, Inc., New York, 1957.

Smith, Adam: *Considerations concerning the First Formation of Languages*, *The Philological Miscellany*, vol. I, 1761.

Snyder, A. D.: *Coleridge on Logic and Learning*, Yale University Press, New Haven, Conn., 1929.

Steinthal, H.: *Grammatik, Logik und Psychologie*, Berlin, 1855.

———: *Gedächtnissrede auf Humboldt an seinem hundertjahrigen Geburtstage*, Berlin, 1867.

Teuber, H. L.: "Perception," in J. Field et al. (eds.), *Handbook of Physiology-Neurophysiology*, American Physiological Society, Washington, D. C., 1960, vol. III.

Troubetzkoy, N. S.: "La phonologie actuelle," *Psychologie de langage*, Paris, 1933.

Vaugelas, Claude Favre de: *Remarques sur la langue françoise*, 1647.

Veitch, J.: *The Method, Meditations and Selections from the Principles of Descartes*, William Blackwood & Sons, Ltd., Edinburgh, 1880.

Wellek, R.: *Kant in England*, Princeton University Press, Princeton, N.J., 1931.

Whitehead, A. N.: *Science and the Modern World*, Macmillan, 1925.

Whitney, W. D.: "Steinthal and the Psychological Theory of Language," *North American Review*, 1872; reprinted in *Oriental and Linguistic Studies*, Scribner, Armstrong and Co., New York, 1874.

Wilkins, John: *An Essay towards a Real Character and a Philosophical Understanding*, 1668.

Wittgenstein, L.: *Tractatus Logico-philosophicus*, 1922; new trans. D. F. Pears and B. F. McGuiness, Routledge & Kegan Paul, Ltd., London, 1961.

———: *Blue and Brown Books*, Harper & Row, Publishers, Incorporated, New York, 1958.